fP

DAILY READINGS FROM

Become a
Better
You

90 Devotions
for Improving Your Life
Every Day

JOEL OSTEEN

FREE PRESS
New York   London   Toronto   Sydney

FREE PRESS
A Division of Simon & Schuster Inc.
1230 Avenue of the Americas
New York, NY 10020

First Free Press hardcover edition October 2008

FREE PRESS and colophon are trademarks of Simon & Schuster, Inc.

For information about special discounts for bulk purchases,
please contact Simon & Schuster Special Sales at 1-800-456-6798
or business@simonandschuster.com.

Manufactured in the United States of America

1   3   5   7   9   10   8   6   4   2

Library of Congress Cataloging-in-Publication Data is available.

ISBN-13: 978-1-4165-7307-4
ISBN-10: 1-4165-7307-0

INTRODUCTION

ARE YOU LIVING BETTER today than you were yesterday? Will you enjoy your life tomorrow more than you are enjoying it today?

You can!

Whether life is going well for us or collapsing right before our eyes, we all want to be better. We want to be more effective in our lives. We want to know God better; we want to be better spouses and parents, better lovers, better encouragers, better community leaders, better employees, and better bosses and managers. None of us gets up in the morning and says, "You know, today I really want to do worse than I did yesterday!" No, God put something deep down inside us that evokes a desire to be more like Him. In our inner being, we hear a voice saying, *You were born for better than this; you are meant to live at a higher level than you are currently. Don't be satisfied with less. You can be better.*

The question is: "How? What must I do to become a better me?"

Today, many people are developing a greater vision for their futures and are experiencing more of God's blessings and favor. But even if you are living your best life now, it is important that you do not become stagnant. God always wants to increase us, to do more in and through us. He always wants to take us deeper into self-discovery and then raise us to a higher level of living. He didn't create us to be average. He doesn't want us to settle for "good enough." He wants us to keep stretching, to keep pressing forward into the next level.

In *Become a Better You,* my goal was to help you look inside yourself and discover the priceless seeds of greatness that God has placed within you. I showed you 7 keys that you can use to unlock those seeds of greatness, allowing them to burst forth in an abundantly blessed life. These keys are not complicated or difficult; in fact, their sheer simplicity often causes them to elude many people's notice. Nevertheless, they are 7 key principles that have helped shape me and continue to keep me expecting good things in my personal life, in my relationships, in my family, and in my career.

I know these principles work, because I have experienced them firsthand in my own life.

So I decided to put together a 90-day reading presentation of the encouraging principles in *Become a Better You* to help you gradually develop a habit of becoming a better you each day.

Let me remind you that these devotionals are not meant to be full treatments of passages of Scripture. I am usually highlighting a specific point from the Bible that will inspire wholehearted love and worship of God. Hopefully the slower pace of these devotional readings will encourage you to immerse yourself in God's Word and see all the practical guidance God has to give you.

These daily readings from *Become a Better You* have been selected to emphasize the 7 keys that form the structure of the book. But I've added several features that I'm convinced will help you apply and live out the truth that God wants you to know. Each devotional includes:

- Scripture Reading to Become a Better You—these passages will sometimes relate directly to the key being described, and in other instances the Scripture reading will provide necessary background for accurately understanding the truth you are studying. Please don't neglect these brief selections from God's Word if you want to gain the most benefit from this book.

- Key verse—usually chosen from the Bible reading that expresses the theme of the devotional.
- Devotional Excerpt from *Become a Better You*—a couple of pages of lessons and stories that I believe will encourage and uplift you.
- Today's Prayer to Become a Better You—some suggestions that will help you express your heart's responses and set the stage for you to share your prayer requests, desires, gratitude, and fresh commitments to God. Feel free to adapt these prayers and make them your own; take a few moments to have a personal conversation with your heavenly Father.
- Today's Thought to Become a Better You—this is not just a sentence for you to read and brush aside; it's a thought for you to think about today. God's Word tells us that our thinking patterns become our acting patterns. The way we talk to ourselves greatly influences the way we act. Today's Thoughts will encourage you to agree with what God thinks of you throughout the day!

As I already mentioned, there are 90 readings in this book. If you take them at the one-a-day pace I'm suggesting, it will take you three months to make your way through these pages. I'm convinced that by the end of the next 90 days, you will have become a noticeably better you. Your life can be transformed and renewed as you allow God's Word to refresh you and reshape your thinking, speaking, and daily activities. May this devotional book be another instrument God uses to help you become a better you!

Joel Osteen

PART ONE

KEEP PRESSING FORWARD

YOU CAN STRETCH!

SCRIPTURE READING TO BECOME A BETTER YOU   John 14:1–14

I tell you the truth, anyone who believes in me will do the same works I have done, and even greater works, because I am going to be with the Father.

JESUS SPEAKING IN JOHN 14:12

THE FAMOUS ARCHITECT Frank Lloyd Wright designed many beautiful buildings, homes, and other magnificent structures. Toward the end of his career, a reporter asked him, "Of your many beautiful designs, which one is your favorite?"

Without missing a beat, Frank Lloyd Wright answered, "My next one."

Frank Lloyd Wright understood the principle of stretching, constantly pressing forward, never being satisfied simply with past successes. The entire world is waiting for your next adventure.

Too many people are living far below their potential. They have many gifts and talents and so much more going for them. But they've gotten comfortable, settled where they are, and lately become too easily satisfied.

I often hear people making excuses for stagnating in their personal growth:

"I've achieved as much as most."

"Compared to other people, I'm doing pretty well in my career."

"I've gone as far as my parents did."

That's great, but God wants you to go further. He's a progressive

God, and He wants every generation to be increasing in happiness, success, and significance. No matter where we are in life, God has more in store. He never wants us to quit growing. We should always be reaching for new heights in our abilities, in our spiritual walk, in our finances, careers, and personal relationships. We all have areas where we can come up higher. We may have achieved a certain level of success, but there are always new challenges, other mountains to climb. There are new dreams and goals that we can pursue.

God never performs His greatest feats in your yesterdays. God wants you to be more blessed tomorrow than you are today.

No doubt, God has already done a lot in your past. He's opened doors for you that nobody else could open. Maybe He's given you a wonderful family and home. Perhaps He's caused you to be promoted, given you favor with your employer or supervisors. That is marvelous, and you should thank God for all that He has done for you. But be careful: Sometimes when you are enjoying life, it is easy to become complacent, to get satisfied, and think, *Yes, God's been good to me. I can't complain. I've achieved my goals; I've reached my limits.*

But God never performs His greatest feats in your yesterdays. He may have done wonders in the past, but you haven't seen anything yet! The best is yet to come. Don't allow your life to become dull. Keep dreaming, hoping, and planning for new projects, experiences, and adventures with God.

I've discovered that God likes to outdo Himself. He wants to show His favor in your life in greater ways today than He did yesterday. He wants you to be more blessed tomorrow than you are today.

He intends for you to have a greater impact on the world than you have had. That means if you're a teacher, you haven't taught your best lesson yet. If you're a builder, you haven't built your best home yet. If you're a businessperson, you haven't negotiated your best deal yet. It's time to get your hopes up; enlarge your vision, and get ready for the new things that God has on the horizon. Your best days are not behind you. They're in front of you.

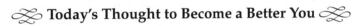 Today's Prayer to Become a Better You

Father, I want to have my vision stretched—I want to be stretched by You! I no longer want the world outside me or my thoughts within me to determine my limitations. I'm trusting You to help me become the better me You already see.

Today's Thought to Become a Better You

God is going to outdo Himself in my life.

DESIGNED FOR BETTER

SCRIPTURE READING TO BECOME A BETTER YOU   Genesis 3:1–19

"Who told you that you were naked?" the LORD God asked.

GENESIS 3:11

OUR POTENTIAL has been put in us by our Manufacturer, our Creator, Almighty God. Whether we use it or not does not diminish it, but it does impact our futures. The events of your past do not reduce your potential. How somebody has treated you or what he or she said about you doesn't change your potential. Maybe you've been through some disappointments or have had some unfair things happen in your life. None of that affects your potential, which has been put in you permanently by the Creator of the universe. When we believe, we take a step of faith and stretch ourselves; that's when we start to tap into it. That's when we'll rise higher.

The capability is in you. The real question is: Are you willing to break free from your self-imposed limitations and start stretching to the next level?

Too often, we allow experiences from the past to keep us from pressing forward. Perhaps a business partner, a coach, a relative, or a friend said, "Hey, do you really think you can do that? Maybe that opportunity is not right for you. What if you try and fail? What if it doesn't work out?"

A young woman named Sherry came to me for advice. She had tolerated an abusive relationship for years in which she was repeatedly told, "You can't do anything right. You're so slow. You're not attractive." After hearing that for so long, it had totally beaten her down physically, emotionally, and spiritually. She had no joy, little confidence, and extremely low self-esteem.

I told her what I'm telling you: Your value, your gifts, and your talents have been put in you by Almighty God. And it doesn't matter what anyone else has spoken over you. The good news is, God has the final authority. He says you have a treasure on the inside. He says you have a gift. He says you are valuable. You've got to quit playing that old tune; put on a new one. You need to be dwelling on thoughts like:

I am creative. I am talented. I am valuable. I have a bright future. My best days are still out in front of me. You have to get your mind going in this new direction, because dwelling on negative thoughts about yourself will keep you from becoming all God has created you to be.

Regardless of who has spoken negative words into your life—a parent, a spouse, a coach, or a teacher—you must cast those words down. Words are powerful. They can create barriers in your heart and mind.

Too many people don't have the confidence and the self-esteem they should have because they're constantly dwelling on negative thoughts about themselves. I don't say this arrogantly, but in my mind, all day long I try to remind myself: *I am anointed. I am creative. I am talented. I am successful. I have the favor of God. People like me. I'm a victor and not a victim.*

Try it! If you go around thinking those kinds of thoughts, low self-esteem, lack of confidence, or inferiority won't have a chance with you. Throw your shoulders back, put a smile on your face, and be looking for opportunities to stretch into the next level.

Back in the Garden of Eden, after Adam and Eve ate the forbidden fruit, they hid. In the cool of the day, God came to them and said, "Adam, Eve, where are you?"

They said, "God, we're hiding because we are naked."

I love the way God answered them. He said, "Adam, who told you you were naked?" In other words, "Who told you that something was wrong with you?" God immediately knew the Enemy had been talking to them.

> Throw your shoulders back, put a smile on your face, and be looking for opportunities to stretch into the next level.

God is saying to you today, *Who told you that you don't have what it takes to succeed? Who told you that the best grades you could make in school would be Cs rather than As? Who told you that you are not attractive enough to succeed in your personal relationships or talented enough to flourish in your career? Who told you that your marriage is never going to last?*

Who told you that something was wrong with you?

Those are lies from the Enemy. You need to reject those ideas and discover what God says about you.

"Well, I don't think I could ever get this promotion, Joel."

Who told you that? God said, "No good thing will I withhold when you walk uprightly."

"Well, I don't think I'll ever get married, Joel. I haven't had a date in so long I don't think I'll ever find someone who would love me for who I am and with whom I would be compatible."

Who told you that? God said, "When you delight yourself in Him, He will give you the desires of your heart."

"Well, I don't think I could ever be in management. I don't think I could be a leader."

Who told you that? God says, "You can do all things through Christ." The potential is inside you. It doesn't change just because you don't believe it or just because you've been through some negative experiences in the past. It has been deposited in you permanently by the Creator of the universe. Scripture says, "God's gifts and His callings are irrevocable" (see Romans 11:29). That means God is never going to take back the potential He has poured into you. He's never going to say, "I'm tired of dealing with you. You've tried and failed too many times. You've made so many mistakes. Let me just have the gifts back."

No, those gifts, and the calling on your life, will be with you till the day you leave this earth. But it is up to you to decide whether you tap into them and use them or not.

 Today's Prayer to Become a Better You

Father, I know I have to be careful to whom I am listening. I realize I can even tell myself lies. So, I want to hear Your words over the barrage of messages that seek to control and bind me. I want to live by Your design.

Today's Thought to Become a Better You

No good thing will God withhold when I walk uprightly.

IF YOU ONLY KNEW

Scripture Reading to Become a Better You   John 4:1–42

Jesus replied, "If you only knew the gift God has for you and who you are speaking to, you would ask me, and I would give you living water."

JOHN 4:10

In John 4, Jesus met a woman at a well in Samaria, and He asked her for a drink of water. She was surprised, because back then, the Jews didn't have anything to do with the Samaritans. She said, "How can you ask me for a drink?"

Jesus said, "If you knew who I was, you would ask me for a drink, and I would give you living water."

The woman thought Jesus was talking about literal water. She said, "Sir, you don't even have anything with which to draw water. You don't have a bucket, and the well is deep. How can you possibly give me water?"

I wonder how many times God tells us that He wants to do something great in our lives, that we are going to be healthy and well, that we are going to get out of debt. We feel it strongly, but like the woman at the well, we start thinking about what we don't have and all the obstacles in our path, and before long we've talked ourselves out of God's best.

"That could never happen for me. I don't have the education; I don't have the talent; I don't have the discipline. I'll never break this addiction; I'll never accomplish my dreams." No, you must quit looking at what you don't have and start believing that all things are possible.

I never dreamed that I'd be doing what I am doing today, encouraging people around the world. For seventeen years, my father tried to get me to speak at our home church, but I had no desire. I'm naturally quiet and reserved and would much prefer working behind the scenes.

But when my father went to be with the Lord, I knew I was supposed to step up. Although I had never preached before, never had been to seminary, and

> The key is to get your eyes off your problems and onto your God.

had no formal training, I said, "God, I'm not going to look at what I don't have. I'm looking unto You. I know in my weakness, You show up the strongest." I took that step of faith, and God has taken me places I never dreamed of.

He can do the same for you. Don't get stuck in a rut in your attitude, your career, or your marriage. You have incredible potential within you—much more than you may realize! God is not limited to the laws of nature. He can do what human beings cannot. The key is to get your eyes off your problems and onto your God.

When God puts a dream in your heart, it may look impossible in the natural. Every voice may tell you it will never happen. "You'll never break that addiction. You'll never accomplish your dreams. You'll never be happy." But if you will believe and remain faithful and expect good things, you, too, can defy the odds.

I talked to a famous tightrope walker who comes from a family of seven generations of circus entertainers. I asked him, "What is the key to walking on the tightrope? You make it look so easy."

He said, "Joel, the secret is to keep your eyes fixed on where you are going. You never look down. Where your head goes, that's where your body is going too. If you look down, there's a good chance you will fall. So you always have to look to where you want to be."

It's the same principle in life. Some people are always looking back, focused on their hurts and pains. Other people are looking down, living in self-pity, and complaining that life is not fair. The key to rising higher is to keep looking to where you want to go. Dream big dreams! Don't focus on where you are today; keep a positive vision, and see yourself accomplishing your goals and fulfilling your destiny.

✑ Today's Prayer to Become a Better You ✑

Father, like You did for the woman at the well, please open my eyes to see what You have already placed within me for Your purposes. I long to enjoy the potential You have given me.

✑ Today's Thought to Become a Better You ✑

Only God knows the full extent of my potential.

DIRECTION THROUGH REJECTION

SCRIPTURE READING TO BECOME A BETTER YOU 2 Corinthians 4:7–18

We now have this light shining in our hearts, but we our-selves are like fragile clay jars containing this great trea-sure. This makes it clear that our great power is from God, not from ourselves.

2 CORINTHIANS 4:7

TOO OFTEN, when we suffer some kind of rejection or disappoint-ment, we get so discouraged that we settle right where we are. "I guess it wasn't meant to be," we rationalize. Or "I thought I could go out with that attractive person, but maybe I am not good-looking enough." Or "I thought I could get the promotion, but I tried and failed. Maybe I don't have the talent. It didn't work out."

When disappointment or rejection knocks you down, get back up and go again. We give up too easily on our dreams. We need to understand that just as God supernaturally opens doors, sometimes God supernaturally closes doors. And when God closes a door, it's always because He has something better in store. So just because you've come to a dead end, that's not the time to give up. Find a dif-ferent route and keep pressing forward.

Often, out of our greatest rejection comes our greatest direction. When you come to a closed door or something doesn't work out in your life, instead of seeing that as the end, regard that as God nudg-ing you in a better direction. Yes, sometimes it's uncomfortable;

sometimes we may not like it. But we cannot make the mistake of just sitting back and settling where we are.

Back in 1959, my father was the pastor of a successful church with a thriving congregation. They had just built a beautiful new sanctuary, and my father had a bright future. About that time, my sister Lisa was born with something like cerebral palsy. Hungry for a fresh touch from God, my dad went away for a while and got alone with God. He searched the Scriptures in a new way, and he began to see how God was a good God, a healing God, and that God could still perform miracles today. My dad went back to his church and preached with a new fire, a new enthusiasm. He thought everybody would be thrilled, but the congregation's reaction was just the opposite. They didn't like his new message. It didn't fit in with their tradition. After suffering much persecution, heartache, and pain, my father knew the best thing for him to do was leave that church.

Out of our greatest rejection comes our greatest direction.

Naturally, my dad was disappointed. He didn't understand why such a thing should happen. But remember, out of rejection comes direction. When one door closes, God is about to open up a bigger and a better door.

My father went down the street to an abandoned feed store. There, he and ninety other people formed Lakewood Church on Mother's Day, 1959. The critics said it would never last, but today, nearly fifty years later, Lakewood Church has grown to become one of the largest churches in America and is still going strong.

I don't believe that my father would have enjoyed the ministry he had, and I don't believe he would have become all God created him to be, if he would have stayed in that limited environment. Here's a key: The dream in your heart may be bigger than the environment in which you find yourself. Sometimes you have to get out of that environment in order to see your dream fulfilled.

Consider an oak tree. If you plant it in a pot, its growth will be limited. Once its roots fill that pot, it can grow no further. The problem is not with the tree; it is with the environment. It is stifling growth. Perhaps you have bigger things in your heart than your present environment can facilitate. That's why, at times, God will stir you out of a comfortable situation. When you go through persecution and rejection, it's not always because somebody has it in for you. Sometimes, that's God's way of directing you into His perfect will. He's trying to get you to stretch to the next level. He knows you're not going to go without a push, so He makes it uncomfortable for you to stay where you are

The dream
in your heart
may be bigger than the
environment in which
you find yourself.

currently. The mistake we make at times is getting negative and sour; we focus on what didn't work out. When we do that, we inhibit the opening of new doors.

A few years ago, Lakewood Church was trying to buy some property on which we could build a new sanctuary. We had looked for months and finally had found a wonderful one-hundred-acre tract of land. We were so excited. However, the day we were to close the deal, it was sold to another group.

I was terribly disappointed, and I had to tell myself, "Joel, God has closed this door for a reason. He has something better in store." Sure, I was down, and I admit that I was discouraged, but I had to shake that off and say, "No, I'm not settling here. I'm going to keep pressing forward."

A few months later, we found another nice piece of property. It would have worked as well, but a similar series of events transpired and the owner refused to sell it to us. Another disappointment. I didn't understand it, but I said, "God, I'm trusting you. I know your ways are not my ways. This doesn't seem right. It doesn't seem fair. But I'm going to stay in an attitude of faith and keep expecting good things."

Not long after that, the door to the Compaq Center, a sixteen-thousand-seat sports arena, opened up in downtown Houston, right in the middle of one of the busiest sections of the city. Then it became clear why God had closed the other doors. Had we purchased either of those properties, those choices might have kept us from God's best.

Throughout life, we're not always going to understand everything that happens. But we've got to learn to trust God. We've got to believe that He has us in the palm of His hand; that He is leading and guiding us, that He always has our best interests at heart.

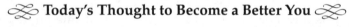 **Today's Prayer to Become a Better You**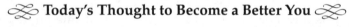

Father, I'm trusting You. I know Your ways are not my ways. Things may not seem right or fair, but I'm going to stay in an attitude of faith and keep expecting good things from You. Please stretch me in Your direction.

Today's Thought to Become a Better You

God already knows the good He has planned next for me.

STEP INTO YOUR FUTURE

Scripture Reading to Become a Better You   Jeremiah 29:4–14

*"I know the plans I have for you," says the LORD.
"They are plans for good and not for disaster, to give you
a future and a hope."*

Jeremiah 29:11

Years ago, I went into a government building that had two sets of double doors spaced about fifteen feet apart. The doors opened automatically as I approached, but for security reasons, when I went through the first set of doors, I had to let them close tightly before the next set of doors would open in front of me. As long as I stayed at the first set of doors, the second set would not open.

In many ways, life operates in a manner similar to those automatic doors. You have to let go of your disappointments, let go of your failures, and let those doors totally close behind you. Step forward, into the future that God has for you, knowing there's nothing you can do about past disappointments. You cannot change the past, but you can do something about the future. What's in front of you is far more important than what is behind you. Where you are going is more significant than where you came from or where you have been.

If you will have the right attitude, you will give birth to more in the future than you've lost in the past. Quit looking back. This is a new day. It may seem like your dreams have died, but God can resurrect your dead dreams or give you brand-new ones. He is a supernatural God, and when we believe in Him, all things are possible.

God has not given up on you; He knows that He put seeds of greatness in you. You have something to offer that nobody else has. He's given you noble dreams and desires. Too often, however, we allow adversities, disappointments, and setbacks to deter us, and before long, we find that we're not pressing forward anymore. We're not stretching; we're not believing we will rise any higher in life.

You will give birth to more in the future than you've lost in the past.

Ironically, some of the most gifted, talented people go through some of the most unfair, unfortunate experiences: divorce, abuse, neglect. And it's easy for such a person to think, *Why is this happening to me? What did I do to deserve any of this?*

Unfortunately, the Enemy knows something about what's on the inside of you, as well. He knows the potential you're carrying, so he does everything he can to keep that seed from taking root. He doesn't want your gifts and talents to flourish. He doesn't want you to accomplish your dreams. He wants you to live an average, mediocre life.

But understand this: God did not create any person without putting something extremely valuable on the inside. Life may have tried to push you down through disappointments or setbacks. In the natural, you don't know how you could rise any higher. You don't see how you're ever going to be happy. But you need to dig your heels in and say, "I know what I have on the inside. I'm a child of the Most High God. I'm full of His can-do power, and I'm going to rise up to become everything God has created me to be."

The apostle Paul urged his young understudy, Timothy, "Stir up the gift within you." Similarly, you need to stir up your gifts, talents, dreams, and desires—in short, the potential within you. Maybe these qualities and traits are buried beneath depression and discouragement, or obscured by negative voices of people telling you that you can't; beneath weaknesses; beneath failures or fears.

But the good things of God are still there. Now you've got to do your part and start digging them out. Step boldly into your future knowing God will never leave you or forsake you.

❧ Today's Prayer to Become a Better You ❧

Father, You have promised me a future and a hope. You have already given me so much. As Your child, I confidently step forward knowing You have prepared me and prepared a way for me. You have filled me with blessing. I'm walking in Your favor today.

❧ Today's Thought to Become a Better You ❧

I'm full of God's can-do power, and I'm going to rise up to become everything He has created me to be.

THE NEXT NEW THING

His anger lasts only a moment, but his favor lasts a lifetime! Weeping may last through the night, but joy comes with the morning.

Psalm 30:5

You may have already endured more than your share of unfair, negative experiences. But know this: God wants to do a new thing. He wants to give you a new beginning. Don't give up. Don't go around thinking you've peaked, that you've reached your limits in life. "Well, Joel, you don't know my situation. I've gone as far as my education can take me. You don't know my struggles."

No, I may not know any of that. But I do know our God, and He is all-powerful. He has more in store for you. My questions for you are: Can you perceive it? Can you make room for it? The first place it starts is in your thinking. If your thinking is limited, then your life is going to be limited.

"But, Joel, I've gone through bankruptcy. I've tried and failed." Well, let it go. This is a new day.

"My marriage didn't work out. I'm so disappointed. I never thought that I'd be in this situation at this point in my life."

That's unfortunate, but it's not the end. When one door closes, God will always open another. If all the doors close, He'll open a window! God always wants to give you a fresh beginning. He still has a great plan for your life. Do you know when that's going to happen? It will commence the moment you quit looking back, when you quit grieving over what you've lost. Nothing will keep you from the good things of God as much as living in the past.

You may feel that life has knocked you down through disappointments or other unfair situations. But whatever you do, don't stay down. Get back up again, dust yourself off. If you can't find anybody to encourage you, learn to encourage yourself. Get up in the morn-

If all the doors close,
God will open
a window!

ing, put your shoulders back, look in the mirror, and say, "I've come too far to stop now. I may be knocked down, but I'm not knocked out. I'm going to get back up again. I know I'm a victor, not a victim."

You must keep yourself stirred up if you're going to see these new doors open. Keep looking for the good things that God is going to do next. I know too many people who are living in the land of "good enough."

No, don't ever let "good enough" be good enough. Keep pressing. Keep believing. You were not made to be average; you were made to excel. You were made to leave your mark on this generation. At the start of each new day, remind yourself: *I am talented. I am creative. I am greatly favored by God. I am equipped. I am well able. I will see my dreams come to pass.* Declare those statements by faith, and before long you will begin to see them in reality.

Understand that throughout life we will always have forces opposing us, trying to keep us from becoming all God has created us to be. And many times, the adversities, the unfair situations, are the results of the Enemy's efforts, attempting to discourage us and deceive us into giving up on our dreams. You may feel as if you're at an empty place in life today. Not much is going your way. You've been through severe difficulties. But God wants to restore you, encourage you, fill you with His hope. He wants to resurrect your dreams. He wants to do a new thing.

Continually remind yourself that you have a gift on the inside. You are talented. You are creative. That's exactly why the Enemy is trying to push you down, to keep your gifts, your creativity, your joy, your smile, your personality, and your dreams from ever seeing the light of day. He would love for them to lie dormant your whole lifetime. Thank God, it's not up to the Enemy; it's up to you.

Thank God, it's not up to the Enemy; it's up to you.

Granted, you may have gotten off to a rough start in life. You may have had more than your share of unfair things happen. But it's not how you start that counts. It's how you finish. Shake off the past; shake off discouragement. Remind yourself that God is still in complete control of your life. If you'll keep your trust in Him, He promises that no weapon formed against you will prosper. Your situation may seem unfair, it may be difficult; it may seem that the forces working against you are winning momentarily, but God said He'd turn your circumstances around and use them to your advantage.

Don't get complacent. Don't let "good enough" be good enough. Keep yourself stirred up. The forces that are for you are greater than the forces that are against you. Scripture says, "Weeping may endure for a night, but joy is coming in the morning" (see Psalm 30:5). No matter what tomorrow morning holds, you can expect God to bring you joy.

❧ Today's Prayer to Become a Better You ❧

Father I believe that You want to do something new in my life, and I will do my part. Guide me, and remind me not to settle for "good enough" but to continuously reach out for more of the good You have in store for me.

⁂ Today's Thought to Become a Better You ⁂

I'm looking with joy for God's new thing in my life.

WAVING AT THE REARVIEW MIRROR

SCRIPTURE READING TO BECOME A BETTER YOU   Joshua 14:6–13

> *My servant Caleb has a different attitude than the others*
> *have. He has remained loyal to me, so I will bring him*
> *into the land he explored. His descendants will possess*
> *their full share of that land.*
>
> NUMBERS 14:24

THE CAR YOU DRIVE has a large windshield, but only a relatively small rearview mirror. The implication is obvious: What happened in your past is not nearly as important as what is in your future. Where you are going is much more important than where you've been. If you stay focused on the past, you're liable to miss numerous excellent opportunities ahead.

How do we let go of the past? First, discipline your thoughts to stop thinking about it. Quit talking about it. Quit reliving every negative experience.

If you have been through a loss or one of your dreams has died, of course there's a proper time for grieving. But at some point, you need to get up, dust yourself off, put on a fresh attitude, and start pressing forward in life. Don't let disappointment become the central theme of your life. Quit mourning over something you can't change. God wants to give you a new beginning, but you have to let go of the old before you'll ever see the new. Let that door close behind you and step through the door in front of you.

Maybe you've allowed other people to convince you that you're never going to rise higher, that you will never see your dreams come to pass. It's been too long. You've messed up too severely.

Don't believe those lies. Instead, take courage from the Old Testament character Caleb. When Caleb was a young man, he and Joshua were part of an exploratory spy mission to determine the strength of the enemy before God's people moved into the land that God had promised them. Of the twelve spies, only Caleb and Joshua presented a positive report to Moses. They said, "We are well able to take the land." The other ten spies said, "No, Moses, there are giants in the land; the opposition is too formidable; the obstacles to overcome are too large." And the majority tried to talk Moses and the rest of the children of Israel out of pressing forward into the blessings that God promised them. They were all too willing to settle for second best, to dwell for the rest of their lives right where they were. Unfortunately, that group of negative thinkers never did make it into the Promised Land. They spent the next forty years spinning their wheels and wandering around aimlessly in a desert. Eventually, most of them died with their dream still in them, as God raised up an entire new generation of people.

Where you are going is much more important than where you've been.

By then Caleb was eighty-five years old, but he hadn't given up on the dream God had placed in his heart. A lot of people that age would be sitting back in rocking chairs, thinking about the good old days, but not Caleb. He kept himself stirred up, and he kept himself in shape as well. He told Joshua that he was still as strong as he was when the promise first came to him.

Caleb went back to the exact same place; the same mountain that the others had feared to climb. He said, "God, give me this mountain." Caleb was saying in effect "I don't want another place to live. I still have this dream in my heart."

Interestingly, Caleb did not ask for an easy inheritance. In fact, the mountain he claimed had five giants living on it. Surely he could have found a place less fortified, more accessible, or more easily occupied. But Caleb said, "No, I don't care how many obstacles are there. God promised me this place. Although it is forty years later, I'm going to keep pressing; I'm going to keep believing until I see that promise fulfilled."

That's the kind of attitude we need to have. We give up too easily. "Well, I didn't get the promotion I wanted; I guess it's not going to happen."

"My husband and I can't get along. I guess it's over."

No, keep pressing forward, and keep believing. Keep yourself stirred up. You've got the gifts, the talents, and the dreams. Don't allow complacency to keep you from seeing God's promises fulfilled in your life.

✆ Today's Prayer to Become a Better You ✆

Help me remember, Father, that when I look back, I can't see You. You are with me, preparing my future. I want to eagerly look forward to what You have in store for me. Teach me to be as confident as Caleb in trusting You along the way.

✆ Today's Thought to Become a Better You ✆

Nothing I will face today surprises or surpasses the One who is with me.

WHERE ARE YOU?

SCRIPTURE READING TO BECOME A BETTER YOU   Psalm 1:1–2

Oh, the joys of those who do not follow the advice of the wicked, or stand around with sinners, or join in with mockers.

PSALM 1:1

AN IMPORTANT KEY to letting go of the past and reaching your full potential is putting yourself in an environment where the seed of your dreams can grow. I know people who are extremely talented. They have incredible potential. But they insist on hanging around the wrong sorts of people. If you are close friends with people who are lazy and undisciplined, people who don't have great dreams, people who are negative and critical, they will rub off on you. Moreover, that environment in which you place yourself will prevent you from rising any higher. You cannot hang out with negative people and expect to live a positive life. If all your friends are depressed and defeated and have given up on their dreams, make some changes. Let's be honest: You're probably not going to pull them up; more likely, if you continue to spend too much time in their presence, they will pull you down.

Certainly, you love your friends; you can pray for them and try to encourage them to make positive changes in their lives, but some-times the best thing you can do is break away from negative people and put yourself in a healthy, positive, faith-filled environment. This is extremely critical, because it doesn't matter how great the potential in the seed, if you don't put it in good soil, it will not take root and grow.

I've had people tell me, "Joel, I don't know why I'm drawn to abusive people. I get out of one bad relationship and into another one that's twice as bad. I know it's not good for me. But I just can't leave. I'd feel guilty."

There's something called "the gift of good-bye."

I usually answer, "No, you have a responsibility to keep yourself healthy and whole. God has entrusted you with His talents, with His dreams. And it may be painful, but the best thing you can do is get away from somebody who is a constant drag on your spirit. Don't allow somebody to treat you that way. You are extremely valuable. You are made in the image of Almighty God."

"Joel, if I take a stand and set some boundaries, that person may leave, may walk away." In truth, that would be the best thing that could ever happen. I heard somebody say there's something called "the gift of good-bye." That means when somebody who is pulling you down chooses to leave, you may not realize it, but that person just did you a great favor. Don't look back; instead keep looking forward. Get ready for the new thing God wants to do in your life.

Today's Prayer to Become a Better You

Father, I know You are calling me to put myself with those who will encourage me. Help me face the fears that are keeping me from turning away from destructive habits and people.

Today's Thought to Become a Better You

I'm willing to say good-bye to what's not good for me.

TRAVELING COMPANIONS

SCRIPTURE READING TO BECOME A BETTER YOU   1 Samuel 17:1–58

The LORD who rescued me from the claws of the lion and the bear will rescue me from this Philistine!

1 SAMUEL 17:37

IF YOU REALLY WANT to press forward, surround yourself with people who encourage you, people who will build you up. Certainly, you need people who will be honest enough to tell you when you are making a poor choice or a bad decision. Don't surround yourself with a bunch of yes-people. On the other hand, don't tolerate a bunch of negative, critical, "can't do it" people. Sometimes the people who will discourage you the most are the people who are closest to you.

Remember King David? When he was just a boy, he told his older brother Eliab that he wanted to fight the huge Philistine giant, Goliath. Eliab tried to discourage David by putting him down. He said, "David, what are you doing out here on the battlefield? You're supposed to be at home taking care of our father's few sheep." He was really saying, "David, you're never going to do anything great. You don't have what it takes."

Right there, David had to make a crucial choice: Would he believe that negative assessment from his brother, or would he believe what God had put in his heart? He could have said, "Well, maybe my brother is right. He's older than I am, more experienced, more knowledgeable about the obstacles we're facing. I'm just a kid. I don't feel too talented. Maybe I will get killed out there."

But no, David said, "Eliab, I don't care what you say about me. I know who I am. I know what God has placed inside me. I'm going to step out and fulfill my God-given destiny." He did just that, facing and felling the giant with a few pebbles from the brook.

Some people you have to love from a distance.

Isn't it interesting that even Jesus had to leave His hometown of Nazareth because the people there were so filled with unbelief? Jesus knew that if He stayed in that negative environment, it would hold Him back.

You, too, may have family members or relatives who lack vision and can't imagine you achieving greatness. Don't get angry with them. Most likely, they're good people. Love them, and treat them with respect, but understand that you cannot be around them on a daily basis. You have to love them from a distance. Life is too short for you to be pulled down by negative, jealous, cynical people. It doesn't matter how great your gift is or how much potential is locked inside your seeds of greatness—if you don't put that seed in an environment conducive to growth, it will not take root. It will be nearly impossible for your dream to flourish.

You need to hang around other dreamers—not daydreamers, but people with big goals, people who plan to do something significant with their lives. Hang around people who are going to help you become all God created you to be.

God is saying this is a time of new beginnings. Get your fire back. Get your passion back. You may have been sick a long time, but this is your day to get well. You may have struggled with depression and discouragement, but this is the time to break free. You may come from a family of defeat, failure, and negativism, but this is your time to rise above that morass.

Start stretching your faith once again. Get up each morning

expecting good things to happen. And remember, God is on your side. He loves you. He's for you. Scripture says, "If you put your trust in him, you will not be disappointed" (see Isaiah 28:16 and Romans 10:11).

My father often quoted a simple yet profound statement by the American poet Edwin Markham (1852–1940) that sums up the attitude we need: "Ah, great it is to believe the dream as we stand in youth by the starry stream; but a greater thing is to fight life through and say at the end, the dream is true!"

Don't settle for mediocrity; never let good enough be good enough. You, too, will discover that the dream is true!

⸙ Today's Prayer to Become a Better You ⸙

Father, while You are helping me become a person others want to be around, lead me also to a circle of encouragers. Please show me people I need to love closely and those I need to love from a distance.

⸙ Today's Thought to Become a Better You ⸙

I'm going beyond good enough to God's good favor.

THE POWER OF YOUR BLOODLINE

Scripture Reading to Become a Better You   Psalm 139:1–18

You saw me before I was born. Every day of my life was recorded in your book. Every moment was laid out before a single day had passed.

PSALM 139:16

I READ RECENTLY ABOUT some famous racehorses, the kind you might see at the Kentucky Derby or other prestigious horse races. I never realized how much time, effort, and resources went into the making of one of those championship horses. I had always thought that somebody was out riding and one day discovered that a certain horse was fast and gifted. So that person decided to enter the horse in some races. Of course, the development of a champion racehorse takes much more than that. It's no fluke that a horse races in the Kentucky Derby.

In horse racing, the bloodstock agent focuses his attention on the animal's bloodline. He or she will spend months studying a particular line of horses, researching the lineage. The bloodstock agent will examine how the horse's father fared as a racer, how long his stride was, how fast he could run, what size he was, and on and on. The breeders understand that winners don't randomly happen. Winning is in the blood.

Simply to breed one of these world champion thoroughbreds can cost up to half a million dollars. And there's no guarantee that the colt will win. In fact, when that newborn colt is born, his legs are all wobbly, he can barely stand up, and his eyes are glazed. The uninformed observer might say, "Those poor owners wasted their money. That horse couldn't win anything. He looks like an average, ordinary horse."

But the owners know that on the inside, in his blood, that colt has a legacy of championship genes. In fact, he may have a dozen world champions on the inside. It's all in the blood. That's why the owners are not necessarily concerned about the colt's initial weakness.

You come from
a bloodline
of champions.

They don't really care what color he is, how pretty he is, or even how large he is. They know that deep down on the inside, that colt has the blood of a winner.

Friend, God looks at you and me the same way. Our external appearance is irrelevant. It doesn't matter what color your skin is or what your ethnic background is. It doesn't matter how many weaknesses or flaws you have. You were made in the image of God. You come from a long line of champions.

Consider this: Your heavenly Father spoke the galaxies into existence. Your elder brother Jesus defeated the Enemy. Think about some of your natural ancestors:

Moses parted the Red Sea. There's great faith in your bloodline.

David, a shepherd boy, defeated Goliath with only a few pebbles he picked up from a brook. That is courage in your bloodline.

Samson toppled a building. There's supernatural strength in your bloodline.

Daniel spent an entire night in a lion's den and wasn't harmed. Divine protection flows through your bloodline.

Nehemiah rebuilt the walls of Jerusalem when all the odds were against him. Determination and persistence pulsate through your bloodline.

Queen Esther put her life on the line to save God's people. Sacrifice and heroism are in your bloodline.

These are not just random names from the Bible; they are part of an unbroken lineage of faith that comes down today and to your life and mine. What God did in their lives He wants to do in ours.

Do you understand? You come from a bloodline of champions. You are not ordinary; you are a thoroughbred. It doesn't matter what your present condition looks like; you need to know that inside you flows the blood of a winner. On the inside of you are seeds of greatness. Take a better look at your bloodline. On the inside of you is champion after champion. You are the seed of Almighty God.

Your lineage is why you must quit focusing on your weaknesses and get a bigger vision for your life. Understand that God sees you already at the Winner's Circle. He's already seen them putting the roses around your neck. That's what David was talking about when he said, "God, all of my days you ordained before one of them came to be" (see Psalm 139:16). In other words, you may be a mere thirty, forty, or fifty years of age, but God has been working on you for a long time. He had you planned long before you were born. You are extremely valuable; you are not ordinary; you come from great stock. You've been destined to live in victory, destined to overcome, destined to leave your mark on this generation.

❧ Today's Prayer to Become a Better You ❧

Thank You, Father, for Your seed in my life. However others may see me, I'm choosing to see myself as You see me—already in the Winner's Circle You prepared for me.

❧ Today's Thought to Become a Better You ❧

It's in my blood to be better and do better today.

LIVING OUT YOUR HERITAGE

SCRIPTURE READING TO BECOME A BETTER YOU   Ephesians 1:3–11

*Even before he made the world, God loved us and chose
us in Christ to be holy and without fault in his eyes.*

EPHESIANS 1:4

To MOST PEOPLE, famous racehorses don't look much different
from ordinary horses. Certainly they are beautiful animals, but the
average person couldn't ascertain the champion from the merely
well-bred horse. The difference is in the blood. That's what makes
champions extremely valuable.

It's the same way with us. Scripture says we overcome by the
blood of the Lamb, the word of our testimony, and a willingness to
lay down our lives (see Revelation 12:11). Because of what God has
done, every one of us is a thoroughbred.

"But you don't know the life I've led," I hear you saying. "I've
failed here, and I've made mistakes over there, and I still have this
addiction."

That doesn't change your bloodline; it doesn't change what's in
you. You may never have realized how valuable you are. Perhaps
you never realized the price God paid for you. You need to recognize
what you have on the inside. It says in 1 Corinthians 6:20 that you
were bought with a high price. God gave His very best for you, His
only Son. So please don't go around thinking that you are worthless,
that you don't have a future. You are a champion on the inside. It's
in your blood.

Perhaps you have never fully considered what you have on the inside. You may have made mistakes, but don't let your mistakes keep you down. Get back up and go again. Your errors or wrong choices do not change your bloodline. They don't change what's in you. Oftentimes, society will write a person off when he or she fails or makes poor choices, but God is not that way. God sees your potential. He knows what you're capable of being. He's the one who designed you, and He knows that you can still do great things. It's in your blood.

> Your spiritual bloodline is more powerful than your natural bloodline.

God has programmed you with everything you need for victory. That's why every day you can say things like, "I have what it takes. I am more than a conqueror. I am intelligent; I am talented; I am successful; I am attractive; I am an overcomer." God put all those things in your bloodline.

Granted, you may have to overcome some negative elements in your family's natural bloodline, but always remember your spiritual bloodline is more powerful than your natural bloodline. You have been handpicked by Almighty God. You have His royal blood flowing through your veins. Put your shoulders back and hold your head up high, knowing that you have been chosen. You've been set apart before the foundation of the world. Understand your value and shake off inferiority or insecurity. The "champion" is already within you, just waiting to be discovered. It's in your blood.

Where I grew up, folks often described a troublemaker by saying, "Well, he's just got bad blood." Really, there's some truth to that. What's in our bloodlines is extremely important. We all have natural bloodlines flowing from our parents, grandparents, great-grandparents, and other members in our family trees.

But we each also have a spiritual bloodline. The good news is that your spiritual bloodline can override your natural bloodline. Scripture talks about all things becoming new. The old is passed away (see

2 Corinthians 5:17). In other words, we have entered into a new bloodline. When you really understand all God has done for you, and you begin to act on it, then you can rise up out of any adversity; you can overcome anything negative from your past. There's power in your spiritual bloodline.

God is the great architect of the universe. He planned everything and prearranged for you to be here at this particular time in history. That's one reason why we should feel a sense of destiny and value.

Understand that your value is not based on how somebody else has treated you or on how perfect a life you have lived, or even how successful you are. Your value is based solely on the fact that you are a child of the Most High God. No, we're not perfect, we make mistakes; we all have weaknesses. But that doesn't change our value in God's eyes. We are each still the apple of His eye. We are still His most prized possession.

❧ Today's Prayer to Become a Better You ❧

When I call You Father, O God, I realize I'm claiming my spiritual bloodline. Help me to live as Your royal child.

❧ Today's Thought to Become a Better You ❧

I'm the King of kings' child.

YOU'RE ON GOD'S MIND

SCRIPTURE READING TO BECOME A BETTER YOU   Galatians 3:23–29

Now that you belong to Christ, you are the true children of Abraham. You are his heirs, and God's promise to Abraham belongs to you.

GALATIANS 3:29

You MAY HAVE SOME things you wish you could change about yourself, but rather than focus on those areas, take what God has given you and make the most of it. You are valuable to God. I heard somebody put it like this: If God had a refrigerator, your picture would be on it. If God carried a wallet, your photo would be in it. You're on His mind (see Psalm 139:17–18).

You may say, "Joel, I haven't gotten good breaks in life, and my parents struggled with these same problems. I think this is my lot in life."

No, your lot in life is to be a victor and not a victim. Your lot in life is to be happy, healthy, and whole. Sure, you may have some things to overcome in that natural bloodline, but your spiritual bloodline looks very good. Your Father spoke the world into existence. He could have chosen anybody for this time and place, but He chose you. He equipped you and approved you.

I love the scripture that says, "If we belong to Christ, we are Abraham's seed, and heirs according to the promise" (see Galatians 3:29). That means we can all experience the blessings of Abraham. If you study Abraham's record, you'll discover that he was prosperous, healthy, and lived a long, productive life. Even though he didn't always make the best choices, he enjoyed God's blessings and favor.

No matter how many mistakes you've made, you need to know that on the inside, you have the seed of Almighty God. Your attitude should be, "I may have a lot to overcome, people may have tried to push me down, maybe I didn't get the best breaks, but that does not change who I am. I know I can fulfill

God could have chosen anybody for this time and place, but He chose you.

my destiny." You should go out each day expecting good things, anticipating God's blessings and favor. God has planned all of your days for good, not evil.

"I don't really see that happening in my life," you say. "I've endured so much adversity."

Maybe so, but if you will keep pressing forward, if you'll keep believing, God says He'll take those negative experiences and turn them around, and He will use them to your advantage.

Remember, we are called overcomers. That means we're going to have obstacles to overcome. You can't have great victories without having difficult battles. You'll never have a great testimony without going through a few tests. The Enemy always fights the hardest when he knows God has something great in store for you.

If you've had unfair things happen to you, or people have robbed or cheated you, Scripture says that God will bring you out with twice what you had before (see Isaiah 61:7). If you are struggling through tough times, start declaring, "I'm coming out of this experience with twice the joy, twice the peace, twice the honor, twice the promotion." Every day when you get up, declare, "This is going to be a day of victory in my life. I'm expecting God's unprecedented favor. Promotion, favor, increase—they're all on the way."

⧲ **Today's Prayer to Become a Better You** ⧲

Based on Your promises and faithfulness, Father, I'm going to expect good things and anticipate Your favor throughout this day.

⧲ **Today's Thought to Become a Better You** ⧲

I am valuable to God, and I'm on His mind.

TAP INTO GOD'S POWER

SCRIPTURE READING TO BECOME A BETTER YOU   Philippians 3:12–14

I press on to reach the end of the race and receive the heavenly prize for which God, through Christ Jesus, is calling us.

PHILIPPIANS 3:14

I'VE HAD PEOPLE TELL ME, "Joel, I know that someday I'll be happy. I know one day I'll enjoy my life in the sweet by and by."

I appreciate what they are saying, but God wants us to enjoy our lives right here in the nasty now and now. He wants us to have a little heaven on earth, right where we are. One of the reasons Christ came was that we might live an abundant life. You can be happy and free in this life, not simply in heaven one of these days; you can accomplish your dreams before you go to heaven!

How can you do that? By tapping into God's power inside of you.

The Bible says, "Christ has redeemed us from the curse of the law" (see Galatians 3:13). The curse is behind any kind of defeat—sin, mistakes, wrong choices, fear, worry, constant sickness, unhealthy relationships, or bad attitudes. Please understand that those are all things from which you have already been set free. But here's the catch: If you don't appreciate and take advantage of your freedom, if you don't get your thoughts, your words, your attitudes going in the right direction, it won't do you any good.

You may be sitting back waiting on God to do something supernatural in your life, but the truth is, God is waiting on you. You

must rise up in your authority, have a little backbone and determination, and say, "I am not going to live my life in mediocrity, bound by
addictions, negative and defeated. No, I'm going to do as the apostle Paul and start pressing forward. I'm going to take hold of everything God has in store for me."

Many times, we're like little dogs that have been left on their leashes so long that they've gotten used to their limitations. We're conditioned to fail-ure. We may be free, but we're not act-ing free or living free. God has loosed our leashes of addictions, of personal defeats, of bad attitudes. The problem is we're not walking out of them.

> The truth is,
> God is waiting
> on you.

"I've always been this way. I've always had a problem with my
temper. I've always had this addiction," some people lament.

No, you need to realize you have already been set free. Two
thousand years ago, God loosened your collar. Now, it's up to you to
start walking out of it.

How do you go beyond your previous limitations? Change your
attitude. Quit saying, "I can't do it; I'll never be well; I'll always be
in debt. I've got too much to overcome."

Every enemy in your life has already been defeated—enemies of
worry, depression, addiction, financial lack—and you have power
over all of them. The same power that raised Christ from the dead is
inside you. There is nothing in your life that you cannot overcome;
no hurt is too deep that you cannot forgive. You have the power to
let go of the negative things of your past. You may have been
knocked down a thousand times, but you have the power to get back
up again. The medical report may not look good, but you have the
power to stand strong.

Refuse to sit back and accept things that are less than God's best.
Your attitude should be, "I know my chains have been removed; I
know the price has been paid, and even if I have to believe my
whole lifetime, even if I have to stand in faith till the day I die, I'm

not going to sit back and accept a life of mediocrity. I'm going to keep pressing forward."

⤜ Today's Prayer to Become a Better You ⤜

Help me to overcome, Father, the things I've been letting limit my life, and let me press forward beyond them into the life of freedom and favor You designed for me.

⤜ Today's Thought to Become a Better You ⤜

With God I can live beyond my limitations.

OVERCOMING NEGATIVE HISTORY

We are not fighting against flesh-and-blood enemies, but against evil rulers and authorities of the unseen world, against mighty powers in this dark world, and against evil spirits in the heavenly places.

EPHESIANS 6:12

IT IS STARTLING but true: The decisions we make today affect our children and our children's children for multiplied generations. The Bible talks about how the iniquity of the fathers can be passed down for three or four generations. That includes bad habits, addictions, negativity, wrong mind-sets, and other types of iniquities.

Perhaps you are struggling in certain areas right now because people who came before you made poor choices. Many times, you can look back and see the results of those choices somewhere in your family line. It is important that we recognize what has happened and not passively accept these dysfunctional patterns. "Well, this is just the way I am. This poverty and sickness has been in my family for years."

No, you need to rise up and do something about your negative history. It may have been there for years, but the good news is it doesn't have to stay there. You can be the one to put a stop to it. You can be the one to choose the blessing and not the curse.

Understand, if you are struggling with one or more of these things, that does not make you a bad person. You need not mope around guilty and condemned because you have some obstacles to overcome. Many times, it may not even be your fault. Somebody else made the poor choices, and now you have to deal with the repercussions. Nevertheless, be careful that you don't use the sins of others as an excuse to perpetuate negative lifestyle patterns. You have to dig your heels in and do something about it.

One of the first steps to overcoming a problem is to recognize what you're dealing with. Identify it. Don't ignore it. Don't try to sweep it under the rug and hope that it will go away. It won't.

You can be the one to choose the blessing and not the curse.

If you're lazy and undisciplined, don't make excuses; just admit it and say, "I'm going to deal with this." If you have an anger problem, or if you don't treat other people with honor and respect, don't try to convince yourself that everything is okay. Admit your problem and deal with it.

Then practice what the Bible says, "Confess your faults one to another and pray for one another that you may be healed" (see James 5:16). Notice, you must be honest enough with yourself to confess your faults. Notice, too, that you're going to have to find a good mature friend and say, "I need your help. I'm struggling in this area, and I need you to pray with me."

Too often we do just the opposite. We think, *I'm not going to tell anybody about this problem. What would they think of me? I'd be embarrassed.*

Instead, swallow your pride, confess your weakness, and get the help you need so you can be free. It is not easy to admit that we need help, but it is necessary, and it is liberating.

You can beat anything that's come against you. No addiction is too difficult for our God. No stronghold is impenetrable to Him. It doesn't matter how long you've had it, or how many times you've tried and failed, today is a new day. If you will be honest with yourself, recognize what you're dealing with, and find somebody to hold you accountable; then you, too, can start living under the blessing and not the curse. You can free yourself from those negative patterns and start a new pattern of goodness and love to pass along to your descendants.

Also, take responsibility for your actions. God has given you free will. You can choose to change. You can choose to set a new standard. Every right choice you make will overturn the wrong patterns that other people in your family's lineage have made. Every time you resist a temptation, you are one step closer to your victory. You may have a negative history, but you don't have to perpetuate it. We can't change the past, but we can change the future by making right choices today.

You can choose to change.

Put a stop to any of the negative patterns in your family's bloodline. It may have been there for years, but you can be the one to make a difference.

Remember, this is a spiritual battle (see Ephesians 6:10–18). You must take authority over any stronghold that is keeping you in bondage. Recognize what it is, identify it, get it out in the open, and deal with it. As you do, you will see God's blessings and favor in your life, and you will pass down those good things to the generations to follow.

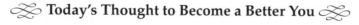

Today's Prayer to Become a Better You

Father, I want to take these steps to deal with my past. Help me identify dysfunctions, confess them, and trust You for the power to overcome them.

Today's Thought to Become a Better You

I'm exchanging a painful past for a hopeful future.

THE GENERATIONAL BLESSING

Scripture Reading to Become a Better You   2 Timothy 1:3–7

I remember your genuine faith, for you share the faith that first filled your grandmother Lois and your mother, Eunice. And I know that same faith continues strong in you.

2 Timothy 1:5

Too often we think only about ourselves. "Well, Joel, it's my life. I know I have some bad habits. I know I'm kind of hot-tempered. I know I don't treat everybody right. But that's okay; I can handle it."

The problem with that kind of thinking is it's not just hurting you; it's making life more difficult for those who come after you. The things that we don't overcome, the issues we leave on the table, so to speak, will be passed down for the next generation to deal with. None of us lives or dies to ourselves. A person's good habits as well as poor choices—the addictions, bad attitudes, and wrong mind-sets—all are passed down.

But the good news is: Every right decision we make, every time we resist temptation, every time we honor God, when we do the right thing, not only are we going to come up higher ourselves, but we're making it a little easier on the generations that will come after us.

Think of it like this: Each of us has a spiritual bank account. By the way we live, we're either storing up equity or storing up iniquity. Equity would be anything good: our integrity, our determination, our godliness. That's storing up blessings. On the other hand, iniquity includes our bad habits, addictions, selfishness, lack of discipline. All of these things, either good or bad, will be passed down to future generations.

Each of us has a spiritual bank account.

I like to look at my life as a few laps in the marathon that our family line is running. When my life is done, I'm going to hand the baton to my children. Contained in that baton will be my physical genes—my traits, hair color, eye color, and size. It will also hold my spiritual and emotional DNA. It will include my tendencies, attitudes, habits, and mind-sets. My children will take the baton, run a few laps, and hand it to their children, and on and on. Every lap that we run with purpose, passion, and integrity is one more lap that can be used for good by those that come after us. In a sense, the laps we run will put future generations further down the road toward significance and success.

Even if you don't have children, you're going to live on through the people you influence. Your habits, attitudes, and what you stand for will all be passed down to somebody.

We need to think about the big picture. I want to leave my family line better off than it was before. I don't want selfishness, addictions, or bad habits to diminish my life. I want everything about my life now to make it easier for those who will come after me.

✇ Today's Prayer to Become a Better You ✇

Thank You, Father, for letting me catch a glimpse of the big picture. I want my life to deposit equity in the legacy I leave for my children. And I will, with Your help.

⚬ Today's Thought to Become a Better You ⚬

I'm making a spiritual equity deposit today.

A PRICELESS LEGACY

Scripture Reading to Become a Better You   Psalm 1:3–6

They are like trees planted along the riverbank, bearing fruit each season. Their leaves never wither, and they prosper in all they do.

PSALM 1:3

IF SICKNESSES and addictions and wrong mind-sets can be passed down in a family, how much more can God's blessings, favor, and good habits be passed down?

I know that much of the favor and blessing on my life did not come to me by my own effort; I didn't accumulate all that I am currently enjoying on my own. It came to me because my father and mother passed it down to me. They left me not just a physical inheritance; they imparted a spiritual inheritance to me as well.

We can build on the past. My father put me forty years down the road when he passed the baton, handing over the ministry of Lakewood Church. My dream is to place my children far, far down the road. And I'm not talking financially; I'm talking about their attitudes, helping them along in their work habits, in their character, and in their walk with God.

We need to remember that the generations are connected. You are sowing seeds for future generations. Whether you realize it or not, everything you do counts. Every time you persevere, every time you are faithful, every time you serve others, you are making a difference; you're storing up equity in your "generational account."

It's easy in life to think, "Well, I'm just a businessman," or, "I'm just a housewife," or, "I'm just a single mom raising my kids, going to work. I'm not going to do anything great. Be realistic."

No, you've got to learn to think more generationally. The fact that you're a hard worker, faithful to your spouse and family, giving it your all— you are sowing seeds for those who come after you. You may not see it all happen in your lifetime. You may very well be sowing a seed for a child or a grandchild to do something great. But don't get discouraged. It's your family legacy. It's not just your life you are changing; you are literally changing your family tree!

Everything you do counts.

My grandmother on my father's side worked extremely hard most of her life. My grandparents were cotton farmers, and they lost everything they had in the Great Depression. They didn't have much money, had little food, and no future to speak of. My grandmother worked twelve hours a day earning ten cents an hour washing people's clothes: a dollar twenty a day.

But Grandmother never complained about her plight. She didn't go around with a poor-me mentality; she just kept doing her best, giving it her all. She was determined and persistent. She may not have realized it, but she was sowing seeds for her children. She passed down hard work, determination, and persistence, which my father built upon. Because Grandmother laid the foundation, Daddy was able to break out of poverty and depression and raise our family to a completely new level.

My grandmother never really enjoyed the blessings and the favor that her descendants did. Had she not been willing to pay the price, my father may never have escaped poverty, and I might not be enjoying the season of usefulness that I am experiencing today.

These days, Victoria and I tend to get a lot of credit for the successful lives we are leading, but we have learned to look back and give credit to whom credit is due: our forebears. Many people in our family lines gave us some help along the way.

My grandmother never received a lot of fanfare during her life-time. She didn't get a lot of glory, but she ran some important laps in our family's race. When she passed that baton, it contained determination, per-sistence, a never-give-up attitude, and a can-do mentality. Now those traits are instilled in our family's legacy. I believe that four or five generations from now,

> It's not just your life
> you are changing;
> you are literally changing
> your family tree!

people in my family line will be better off because of Grandmother Osteen.

⤷ Today's Prayer to Become a Better You ⤶

Father, thank You for those who have given me a faithful her-itage! Help me to remember each day that I can add good to what the next generations will receive.

⤷ Today's Thought to Become a Better You ⤶

I'm adding some persistence to my legacy baton today.

A REAL HEAD START

SCRIPTURE READING TO BECOME A BETTER YOU   2 Samuel 7:1–17

When you die and are buried with your ancestors, I will raise up one of your descendants, your own offspring, and I will make his kingdom strong. He is the one who will build a house—a temple—for my name. And I will secure his royal throne forever.

2 SAMUEL 7:12–13

OFTENTIMES, you may see further than you're going to go personally. God may put something bigger in you than you can accomplish on your own. Don't be surprised if your children or your grandchildren come along and finish what you started. I heard somebody say, "Nothing truly great can ever be accomplished in just one lifetime." At the time, I didn't understand that saying, because obviously, every generation can do something great. But I've learned that sometimes God's plans span more than one generation.

Many times, I heard my father say, "One day we're going to build an auditorium to hold twenty thousand people. One day, we're going to have a big place where we can all come together and worship." My father had the vision, but God used his children to complete it. Nevertheless, had he not stayed faithful—had he not stayed determined and kept that excellent spirit—I don't believe the fulfillment would have come to pass. Daddy sowed the seeds; he paved the way, and my family members—as well as millions of other people—have enjoyed the blessings as a result.

You may have a big dream in your heart. Keep in mind that God may have put that seed in you to get it started. Your children and your grandchildren may take it further than you ever thought possible.

In the Old Testament, King David had a dream to build a permanent temple where God's people could worship. David gathered the supplies, brought in huge cedars from Lebanon, and amassed a fortune in gold and other precious metals. But God never allowed David to build the temple. Instead, God instructed David's son Solomon to construct His house of worship.

> You may have a big dream in your heart. . . . God may have put that seed in you to get it started.

Keep doing your best. God is still in control. In addition, as you continue sowing seeds and living with excellence, know this: You are making a difference. In God's perfect timing, the fruit of your labor will be seen.

Scripture says that God's people left the land better off than it was when they found it (see 1 Chronicles 4:40). That should be our goal as well: I'm going to leave my family with more integrity, more joy, more faith, more favor, and more victory. I'm going to leave my loved ones free from bondage and closer to God.

Maybe you weren't raised by parents who set you up for success by planting positive characteristics in your family line. Possibly you've inherited attitudes of defeat, mediocrity, addiction, and negativity. But, thank God, you can start a new family line. You can be the one to set a new standard.

Somebody has to be willing to pay the price. Somebody has to step up and clear the leftovers off the table. Negative things may have been in your bloodline, but they don't have to stay in your bloodline. All it takes is for one person to rise up and start making better choices. Every right choice you make begins to overturn the wrong choices of those who have gone before you.

Nobody else may have done so, but if you'll make positive changes, one day people in your family line will look back and say, "It was because of this man. It was because of that woman. They were the turning point. We were defeated up till then. We were addicted up to that point. However, look what happened when they came along. Everything changed. We came up higher."

Somebody has to be willing to pay the price.

What happened? The curse was broken and the blessings began. That's what you can do for your family.

❧ Today's Prayer to Become a Better You ❧

Thank You, Father, for small and large dreams. With Your help. I'm making better, healthier, and wiser choices today.

❧ Today's Thought to Become a Better You ❧

I'm making life better for my yet-to-be-born great-grandchildren.

YOUR ENDURING HOUSE

SCRIPTURE READING TO BECOME A BETTER YOU   1 Samuel 25:2–42

Please forgive me if I have offended you in any way. The LORD will surely reward you with a lasting dynasty, for you are fighting the LORD's battles. And you have not done wrong throughout your entire life.

1 SAMUEL 25:28

CERTAINLY EACH OF US is responsible for our own actions, and you and I must work diligently to make use of the opportunities afforded us. But the Bible also indicates that when we have this heritage of faith, we will live in houses that we did not build. We will enjoy vineyards that we didn't plant. God's blessings will chase us down and overtake us. I thank God every day for my parents and grandparents. Because of the way they lived and what they've done, I know I'm not living under a generational curse; I'm living under a generational blessing.

You can do something similar for your family. Money, houses, cars, or other material possessions may be part of your legacy to your children—if you leave those things to your heirs, that's great. Living a life of integrity and excellence that honors God is worth more than all of that. To pass on the favor and blessings of God to your future generations is worth more than anything else in this world.

Don't take the easy way out. Keep doing your best even when it's difficult. Keep loving, giving, and serving. Your faithfulness is noticed in heaven. You are storing up equity for both yourself and generations to come.

First Samuel, chapter 25, relates how David and his men protected the family and workers of a man by the name of Nabal from their enemies. Then one day David sent his men to ask Nabal for some food and supplies. David thought that Nabal would be grateful and that he would freely give David's troops the supplies they requested. But when David's men arrived, Nabal treated them rudely and disrespectfully. He said, "I don't even know who you are. I never asked you to do any of this, so just be on your way. Don't bother me."

To pass on the favor and blessings of God to your future generations is worth more than anything else in this world.

When those men got back and told David how insolently they had been treated, David was furious. He said, "All right, men. Get your swords. We're going to go take care of Nabal. We're going to wipe him out."

But on the way there, David was intercepted by Nabal's wife, Abigail. She had heard about her husband's insulting behavior, so she brought a bountiful supply of gifts and food, hoping to reduce David's anger. She said, "David, my husband is a rude and ungrateful man. He shouldn't have treated you like that." In verse 28, she said, "But David, if you will forgive this wrong, I know that God will give you an enduring house."

I like that phrase "an enduring house." Abigail was saying, "David, I know you have a right to be angry. I know my husband paid you back evil for your good, but if you can overlook it, take the high road, and let it go, I know God will bless you for generations to come. I know He will give you an enduring house."

David swallowed his pride, walked away, and overlooked the offense. He let it go, and God did indeed bless him and his future children as a result.

It may be difficult, but you have the power to overcome the

wrong choices made by your family members in previous generations. Beyond that, you can make life better for the generations that follow you. Every offense that you forgive, every bad habit you break, every victory you win is one less lap for those who come after you. Even if you don't do it for yourself, do it for your children, do it for your grandchildren. Do it so you can have an enduring house.

❧ Today's Prayer to Become a Better You ❧

Thank You, Father, for the hope that I can pass down a godly heritage. Show me those things I'm doing that endanger my legacy, and help me turn away from them.

❧ Today's Thought to Become a Better You ❧

When offenses come today, I will shake them off.

STEP INTO YOUR DIVINE DESTINY

I knew you before I formed you in your mother's womb.
Before you were born I set you apart and appointed you
as my prophet to the nations.

JEREMIAH 1:5

BEFORE YOU WERE BORN, God saw you, and He endowed you with gifts and talents uniquely designed for you. He's given you ideas and creativity, as well as specific areas in which you can excel.

Why, then, do so many people today feel unfulfilled in their lives, merely going to work at some mundane job, trying to earn a living, stuck in a career they don't even like? The answer is simple: They are not pursuing the dreams and desires God has placed within their hearts.

If you are not moving toward your God-ordained destiny, tension and dissatisfaction will always grow in your inner being. They won't go away with time; they will be there as long as you live. I can't think of anything more tragic than to come to the end of life on earth and realize that you have not really "lived," that you have not become what God created you to be. You simply endured an average, mediocre life: You got by, but you lived without passion or enthusiasm, allowing your inner potential to lie dormant and untapped.

I heard somebody say the wealthiest place on earth is not Fort Knox or the oil fields of the Middle East. Nor is it the gold and diamond mines in South Africa. Ironically, the wealthiest places on earth are the cemeteries, because lying in those graves are all kinds of dreams and desires that will never be fulfilled. Buried beneath the ground are books that will never be written, businesses that will never be started, and relationships that will never be formed. Sadly, the incredible power of potential is lying in those graves.

God deposited a gift, a treasure, inside you, but you have to do your part to bring it forth.

A major reason why so many people are unhappy and lacking enthusiasm is that they are not fulfilling their destinies. Understand, God deposited a gift, a treasure, inside you, but you have to do your part to bring it forth.

How can you do that? Simple: Determine that you are going to start focusing on your divine destiny and taking steps toward the dreams and desires that God has placed in your heart. Our goal should be that we're going to live life to the fullest, pursuing our passions and dreams, and when it comes our time to go, we will have used as much of our potential as possible. We're not going to bury our treasures; instead, we're going to spend our lives well.

How do you discover your sense of divine destiny? It's not complicated. Your destiny has to do with what excites you. What are you passionate about? What do you really love doing? Your destiny will be a part of the dreams and desires that are in your heart—part of your very nature. Because God made you, and because He is the one who put those desires within you in the first place, it shouldn't surprise you that your destiny will involve something that you enjoy. For instance, if you really love children, your destiny will probably be connected to something that has to do with kids—teaching, coaching, caring for them, mentoring them. Your destiny will usually follow the dream about which you are most passionate.

As a young man, I spent most of my weekends at Lakewood Church, where my father was the senior pastor. At the time, the church owned some small industrial cameras, and I'd spend all day Saturday playing with the television equipment. I didn't really know how to run it, but I was fascinated by it. I'd turn the camera on and off, unplug it, plug it back in, coil the cables, and get the equipment ready for Sunday. I was passionate about it because it was what came naturally to me.

Looking back, I see now that my love for television production was part of my God-given destiny. God had hardwired that into me before the foundation of the world.

I went to college and studied broadcasting for a year, returned home, and started a full-fledged television ministry at Lakewood Church. Today, I am on the other side of the cameras, and I can see how God was guiding my steps and preparing me for the fulfillment of my destiny.

Maybe you don't like the field in which you are working—you awaken each morning dreading going to your job. The work is meaningless and mundane.

If that sounds like you, it may be time to reexamine what you are doing. You are not meant to live a miserable and unfulfilled life. Make sure that you are in a field that is a part of your destiny. Don't spend twenty-five years in a meaningless existence, doing something you dislike, staying there simply because it is convenient and you don't want to rock the boat. No, step into your divine destiny.

⨎ Today's Prayer to Become a Better You ⨎

Father, I'm eager to discover the destiny You have in mind for me. Help me pay attention to the dreams and desires You've given me.

⨎ Today's Thought to Become a Better You ⨎

What I love to do is a key to my destiny.

THE GIFTED LIFE

Scripture Reading to Become a Better You   Romans 12:1–8

God has given each of us the ability to do certain things well.

ROMANS 12:6 *The Living Bible*

GOD HAS GIVEN YOU certain talents, gifts, or skills—things that you can do well, specific areas in which you excel. Don't take them for granted. It may be in sales or communications or in encouraging people or in athletics or in marketing; whatever it is, don't denigrate it simply because it comes naturally to you. That may well be precisely what God has hardwired into you. It may be an important part of your destiny. Make sure that you explore it to the fullest, keeping in mind that what seems boring to one person may be exhilarating to another for whom that area is part of his or her destiny.

My brother-in-law Kevin is the administrator at Lakewood Church, and he is a tremendous help to our entire staff. Kevin is a detail person, extremely organized and efficient. He plans wisely and uses his time well. It is not merely something he learned at a time-management seminar; it is a God-given gift. (In my opinion, it is not normal to be that organized! But I'm glad that Kevin is.)

When we were overseeing the $100 million renovation of the Compaq Center into Lakewood Church, Kevin knew every detail of the construction project. He knew where every penny was spent, and he could explain why it was spent. Beyond that, he could tell you three other ways that we tried to accomplish the same thing while saving money. Kevin is a detail person.

When Victoria, I, and our children go on vacation with Kevin and Lisa's family, Kevin sends me an advance itinerary. He'll send me my tickets as well as a weather report. He'll send me rental-car information and driving directions. The morning of our flight, he calls to tell me where traffic is backed up on the freeway. One time I got to the airport and realized I had forgotten my driver's license, so now Kevin sends me instructions—in writing—regarding matters that I never even think about. He reminds me to bring my driver's license. He is gifted in being detail oriented.

> You can't do everything well, but you can do *something* well.

Kevin stays in his area of strength. He excels as our administrator. Kevin could think in the back of his mind, *Well, if I could get up there and preach, I'd really be making a difference.* But no. If Kevin got up and preached, we might not need the Compaq Center! He can't preach, and I can't administrate. He's doing what he's good at naturally. He's often told me, "Joel, this job is a dream come true." Kevin loves coming to work every day. He's passionate about it. It's what he's good at. It's a part of his destiny.

You need to be aware of your natural strengths as well and use them to your best advantage and to the benefit of others. It says in Romans 12, verse 6, in *The Living Bible,* "God has given each of us the ability to do certain things well." You can't do everything well, but you can do *something* well. Focus on your strengths, and make sure you are not missing out on your destiny because you are always getting involved in something that doesn't come naturally. When you are truly in your destiny, it is not a constant struggle. It just feels right.

❧ Today's Prayer to Become a Better You ❧

Father, I look forward with joy to settling into what You have destined for me, because it will be the best life I can have.

❧ Today's Thought to Become a Better You ❧

I will pay more attention to what I can do well.

FEELING GOD'S PLEASURE

SCRIPTURE READING TO BECOME A BETTER YOU
1 Corinthians 12:4–11

It is the one and only Spirit who distributes all these gifts.
He alone decides which gift each person should have.
1 CORINTHIANS 12:11

PROVERBS 18:16 SAYS that your gift will make room for you. I'm convinced if you'll get into your destiny, no matter where you are, you won't have any problem getting hired or getting happy. You won't have any problem finding work, friends, or opportunity. In fact, if you'll focus on your strengths and do what you're gifted to do, you'll probably have to turn down opportunities.

If you are not fulfilled, it may well be because you are not pursuing your destiny. Make sure that you are fulfilling the dreams that God has placed in your heart. Are you tapping into the potential that's on the inside? Have you discovered what you do best, what comes naturally? Are you excelling in that area?

If you are called to be a stay-at-home mom and raise your children, do it to the best of your ability. Don't allow society to pressure you into some career simply because your friends are doing it. Recognize your purpose and do it well.

If you are gifted in the area of sales, don't sit behind a desk all day long in a room by yourself. Get into the area of your gifting, and do it to the best of your ability. If you're going to fulfill your destiny, you must do what God hardwired you to do. Make sure you operate in a realm where you are passionate.

One of my favorite old movies is *Chariots of Fire*. In this film, Eric Liddell is a gifted runner whose dream is to compete in the Olympics, but he feels called to be a missionary in China. Yet he knows that God has given him his gift of running. When he runs, he feels that he is dedicating himself to God. In one of the classic lines from the movie, Liddell

Stay in your purpose.

says, "When I run, I feel His pleasure." He was saying, when I do what I know I'm called to do, when I'm using my gifts and talents, when I'm pursuing my destiny, I can feel God smiling down on me.

Another of my favorite lines in the film is when Liddell says, "To win is to honor God." I believe we should live by that same philosophy, striving to excel, pursuing our destiny, becoming the best that we can possibly be, and as we do, we will honor God. If you're called to be a businessman, excel at it and you honor God. If you're called to teach children, excel in it and you honor God. Whatever you are called to do, if you'll do it to the best of your ability and excel at it, you are honoring God.

You may not have yet stepped into your divine destiny. You're still doing many things for which you have little passion and no enthusiasm. It is time to become a better you.

Certainly, you can't just snap your fingers and change careers, but at least examine your life and be aware of how you're spending your time. Are you pursuing your passion? Are you doing what you are good at naturally? If not, why don't you make some changes? Time is short. Find one thing that you're passionate about and start giving yourself to it. And God will lead you one step at a time.

I mentioned earlier how God put the desire in me for television production as a young man. I followed that passion, then when my father went to be with the Lord, I had the desire to step up and pastor the church, and I followed that passion. I can honestly say today that I believe I've stepped into my God-given destiny. I know this is why God put me here; this is why I was born.

Follow God's divine destiny for your life, discover your calling, and stay in your purpose. Make a decision to keep pressing forward, keep believing, and keep stretching until you see your dreams fulfilled. Then one day, you will look back and say with confidence, "This is why God put me here."

Today's Prayer to Become a Better You

With Your help, Father, I will press forward toward the dreams and purpose You have placed within me.

Today's Thought to Become a Better You

I'm stepping toward my God-given destiny.

PART TWO

BE POSITIVE TOWARD YOURSELF

WISE DEAFNESS

I heard a loud voice shouting across the heavens, "It has come at last—salvation and power and the Kingdom of our God, and the authority of his Christ. For the accuser of our brothers and sisters has been thrown down to earth—the one who accuses them before our God day and night."

REVELATION 12:10

IF YOU TRULY WANT to become a better you, it is imperative that you learn to feel good about yourself. Too many people live under condemnation, constantly listening to the wrong voices. The Bible refers to the Enemy as "the accuser of the brethren" who would love for us to live our lives guilty and condemned. He constantly brings accusations against us, telling us what we didn't do or what we should have done. He'll remind us of all our past mistakes and failures.

You lost your temper last week.

You should have spent more time with your family.

You went to church, but you arrived late.

You gave, but you didn't give enough.

Many people swallow these lines with little or no defense. Consequently they walk around feeling guilty, condemned, and extremely discontented with themselves. They go through their days without joy, without confidence, expecting the worst and often receiving it.

Granted, no human being is perfect. We've all sinned, failed, and made mistakes. But many people don't know they can receive God's mercy and forgiveness. Instead, they allow themselves to be beaten up on the inside. They tune in to that voice telling them, *You blew it.*

You messed up. They are so hard on themselves. Instead of believing that they're growing and improving, they believe that voice telling them, *You can't do anything right. You'll never break this habit. You're just a failure.* When they wake up in the morning, a voice is telling them what they did

> There's a time to repent, but there's also a time to shake it off and press forward.

wrong yesterday and how they'll probably do something wrong today. As a result, they become extremely critical toward themselves, and that usually spills over to other people as well.

If we're going to live in peace with ourselves, we must learn to put our foot down and say, "I may not be perfect, but I know I'm growing. I may have made mistakes, but I know I am forgiven. I have received God's mercy."

Sure, we all want to be better human beings, but we needn't beat ourselves up over our shortcomings. I may not have a perfect performance, but I know my heart is right. Other people may not always be pleased with me, but I'm confident that God is.

Similarly, as long as you're doing your best and desire to do what's right according to God's Word, you can be assured God is pleased with you. Certainly, He wants you to improve, but He knows that we all have weaknesses. We all do things that we know in our hearts we shouldn't do. When our human foibles and imperfections poke through our idealism, it's normal to get down on ourselves. *After all,* we tend to think, *we don't deserve to be happy; we have to prove that we're really sorry.*

But no, we should learn to receive God's forgiveness and mercy. Don't allow those condemning voices to play repeatedly in your mind. That will only accentuate a negative attitude toward yourself, which will hinder every area of your life.

Negative accusations take various forms: *You're not as spiritual as you should be. You didn't work hard enough last week.* Or *God can't bless you because of your past.*

Those are all lies. Don't make the mistake of dwelling on that rubbish, not for a moment. Sometimes when I walk off the platform, having spoken at Lakewood and around the world by means of television, the first thought that comes to my mind is, *Joel, that message just wasn't good today. Nobody got anything out of that. You practically put them to sleep.*

I've learned to shake that off. I turn it around and say, "No, I believe it was good! I did my best. I know that at least one person really got something out of it. I did. I thought it was good."

As long as we're doing our best, we don't have to live condemned, even when we make mistakes or fail. There's a time to repent, but there's also a time to shake it off and press forward. Don't live with regrets. Don't go around saying, "Well, I should have done this or that," or, "I should have gone back to college," or, "I should have spent more time with my family," or, "I should have taken better care of myself."

No, quit condemning yourself. Your analysis and observations may be true, but it doesn't do you any good to put yourself down. Let the past be the past. You cannot change it, and if you make the mistake of living in guilt today because of something that happened yesterday, you won't have the strength you need to live this day in victory.

✺ Today's Prayer to Become a Better You ✺

Father, I know You could work a special miracle in my life, and make it hard for me to hear the accusing voices that echo inside me. But even if You don't, help me hear Your voice of mercy and love.

⨎ Today's Thought to Become a Better You ⨎

I'm listening for my heavenly Father's voice in my heart, mind and spirit.

RECEIVING GOD'S MERCY

SCRIPTURE READING TO BECOME A BETTER YOU   Romans 7:14–8:1

Now there is no condemnation for those who belong to Christ Jesus.

ROMANS 8:1

THE APOSTLE PAUL once said, "The things I know I should do, I don't. The things I know I shouldn't do, I end up doing" (see Romans 7:19). Even this great man of God who wrote half the New Testament struggled in this regard. That tells me God does not disqualify me merely because I don't perform perfectly, 100 percent of the time. I wish I did, and I'm constantly striving to do better. I don't do wrong on purpose, but like anyone else, I too have weaknesses. Sometimes I make mistakes or wrong choices, but I have learned not to beat myself up over those things. I don't wallow in condemnation; I refuse to listen to the accusing voice. I know God is still working on me, that I'm growing, learning, and becoming a better me. I have made up my mind that I'm not going to live condemned during the process.

That accusing voice will come to you and tell you, *You lost your temper last week in traffic.*

Your attitude should be, "That's okay. I'm growing."

Well, you said some things yesterday you shouldn't have.

"Yes, that's true. I wish I wouldn't have spoken like that, but I have repented. Now, I know I'm forgiven. I'm going to do better next time."

Well, what about that failure you went through two years ago in your relationship and in your business?

"That's in the past. I've received God's mercy. This is a new day. I'm not looking back; I'm looking forward."

I may have made mistakes, but I know I am forgiven. I know I'm the apple of God's eye.

When we have that kind of attitude, we take away the lethal power of the Accuser. He can't control us when we don't believe his lies.

Perhaps you need to shake off that old guilty feeling. You need to quit listening to the voice that's telling you, *God is not pleased with you. You have too many weaknesses. You've made too many mistakes.*

No, as long as you have asked God to forgive you and you are pressing forward in the direction He wants you to go, you can know with confidence that God is pleased with you. When that accusing voice taunts, *You've blown it; you don't have a future; you're so undisciplined,* don't sit back and agree, "Yeah, that's right."

No, you need to start talking back to the Accuser. You need to rise up in your authority and say, "Wait a minute. I am the righteousness of God. God has made me worthy. I may have made mistakes, but I know I am forgiven. I know I am the apple of God's eye. I know God has great things in store for me."

Scripture tells us to "put on the breastplate of God's approval" (see Ephesians 6:14). That's one of the most important pieces of our spiritual armor. Think about what the breastplate covers. It covers your heart, the center of your being, the way you think and feel about yourself deep inside. If you're going around with that gnawing feeling, thinking, *I don't have much of a future. I've blown it too many times. God couldn't be pleased with me,* I can tell you this: You're listening to the wrong voice. That's the Accuser.

You need to start getting up every morning and saying with confidence: "God is pleased with me. God approves me. God accepts me just the way I am."

⁂ Today's Prayer to Become a Better You ⁂

Father, what a gift! Your approval; Your mercy. I want to live with that loving acceptance and protection wrapped around me forever!

⁂ Today's Thought to Become a Better You ⁂

I know God has great things in store for me.

YOUR FATHER'S FACE

The LORD keeps watch over you as you come and go, both now and forever.

PSALM 121:8

GOD DOES NOT FOCUS on your mistakes or your failures. He does not desire to make your life miserable or to see how much frustration you can take. God wants you to succeed; He created you to live abundantly.

You needn't go through life with that nagging feeling, *God is not pleased with me. I'd be a hypocrite to ask for His help after all the mistakes I've made.*

Quite the contrary, you are the apple of God's eye. You are His prized possession. Nothing you have ever done, or will ever do, can keep God from loving you and wanting to be good to you.

Dare to believe that. Shake off those feelings of guilt and unworthiness. It doesn't please God for us to drag through life feeling like miserable failures, trying to show God how sorry we are for our wrong choices. Instead, recognize that you are His child, that He loves you and would do almost anything to help you. Dust yourself off, straighten up, and throw your shoulders back, knowing that you are forgiven. Declare, "I may have made some mistakes; I may have blown it badly, but I know God is full of mercy and still has a great plan for my life."

Develop this new attitude free from guilt and condemnation

and—most of all—free from the accusing voice. No matter how long it has been lying to you, telling you that you're washed up, that you've made too many mistakes, God still has a great plan for your life. You may have missed Plan A, but the good news is that God has a Plan B, a Plan C, and a Plan D. You can turn your face toward Him, knowing that He has already turned His face toward you.

God's face will always be turned toward you.

My parents often told our family members a poignant story of when my oldest brother, Paul, was just a small boy, before any of us siblings were born. Mother and Dad would put Paul in bed at night and then they'd go get in their own bed. Their room was just a few feet down the hall, and every night, my parents would say, "Good night, Paul."

Paul would answer, "Good night, Mother. Good night, Daddy." One night for some reason, Paul was afraid. After they had said their good nights, a few minutes later, Paul said, "Daddy, are you still in there?"

My father said, "Yes, Paul. I'm still in here."

Then Paul said, "Daddy, is your face turned toward me?"

Somehow, the assurance that Daddy was looking in his direction made Paul feel more secure. He could sleep peacefully knowing that my father's face was turned toward him.

"Yes, Paul, my face is turned toward you."

Paul soon drifted off to sleep, knowing that he was under Daddy's watchful care and protection.

Friend, please know your heavenly Father's face is turned toward you. The good news is that God's face will always be turned toward you, regardless of what you have done, where you have been, or how many mistakes you've made. He loves you and is turned in your direction, looking for you.

Maybe you used to be excited about your life, but along the way, you experienced failures, disappointments, and setbacks. Perhaps those accusatory voices have been nagging at you, keeping you down, discouraged, guilty, condemned. You need to know today that God is running toward you. His face is turned in your direction. He is not an angry, condemning God. He is a loving, merciful, forgiving God. He's your heavenly Father, and He still has a great plan for your life.

✶ Today's Prayer to Become a Better You ✶

Father, I am comforted and encouraged each time I think of Your face turned toward me with acceptance and mercy in Your eyes. Knowing that, I can press on.

✶ Today's Thought to Become a Better You ✶

Nothing can diminish or defeat God's love for me.

LOVING THE ONE IN THE MIRROR

The second [commandment] is equally important: "Love your neighbor as yourself." No other commandment is greater than these.

MARK 12:31

WE ALL HAVE AREAS where we need to improve, but as long as we're pressing forward, getting up each day and doing our very best, we can be assured that God is pleased with us. He may not be pleased with every decision we make, but He is pleased with us. I know it is difficult for some people to believe, but God wants us to feel good about ourselves. He wants us to be secure and to have healthy self-images, but so many people focus on their faults and weaknesses. When they make mistakes, they're extremely critical of themselves. They live with that nagging feeling that chides, *You're not what you're supposed to be. You don't measure up. You've blown it too many times.*

Guess what? God knew you were not going to be perfect. He knew you were going to have weaknesses, faults, and wrong desires—He knew all that before you were even born—and He still loves you!

One of the worst things you could do is to go through life being against yourself. This is a major problem today. Many people have a war going on inside themselves. They don't really like who they are. "Well, I'm slow, I'm undisciplined, I'm unattractive, and I'm not as smart as other people." They focus on their weaknesses, not realizing that this negative introspection is a root cause of many of their difficulties. They can't get along in relationships, they're insecure, they don't enjoy their lives, and it's largely because they're not at peace with who they are.

You can't give away what you don't have.

Jesus said, "Love your neighbor as you love yourself" (see Matthew 22:39). Notice, the prerequisite to loving others is to love yourself. If you don't have a healthy respect for who you are, and if you don't learn to accept yourself, faults and all, you will never be able to properly love other people. Unfortunately, self-loathing destroys many relationships nowadays.

I've met many people who think their spouses are the reason they can't get along in their marriages. Or they're sure that office strife is their coworkers' fault. But the fact is, they have a civil war raging on the inside. They don't like their looks, they don't like where they are in life, or they're upset because they haven't broken a bad habit, and that poison spills out into their other relationships.

Understand, you can't give away what you don't have. If you don't love yourself, you're not going to be able to love others. If you're at strife on the inside, feeling angry or insecure about yourself, feeling unattractive, feeling condemned, then that's all you can give away. On the other hand, if you'll recognize that God is working on you, and in spite of your flaws and weaknesses, you can learn to accept yourself. Then you can give that love away and have healthy relationships.

This basic principle could save your marriage; it could change your relationships with the people around you. You think everybody else is the problem, but before you can make significant progress in life, you must come to peace with who you are. Please recognize that if you're negative toward yourself, it's not only affecting you; it is influencing every relationship you have, and it will affect your relationship with God.

That's why it's so important that you feel good about who you are. You may have some faults. You may have some things you wish you could change about yourself. Well, join the crowd. We all do. But lighten up and quit being so hard on yourself.

I'm not talking about living a sloppy life or having a flippant, unconcerned attitude toward sin and mistakes. The fact that you are reading this book indicates that you want to be better, that you are striving for excellence, and that you have a heart to please God. If that's you, don't live under mounds of condemnation merely because you are still struggling in some areas. When you make mistakes, simply go to God and say, "Father, I'm sorry. I repent. Help me to do better next time." Then let it go. Don't beat yourself up for two weeks, or two months, or two years. Shake it off and move on.

∾ Today's Prayer to Become a Better You ∾

Father, I do want to come to peace with who I am. I don't want to carry around mounds of condemnation when I can repent and live freely in Your love. Thank You for reminding me that You love me!

∾ Today's Thought to Become a Better You ∾

Loving others, including God, begins with loving myself as God loves me.

GOD'S APPROVING LOVE

Scripture Reading to Become a Better You   1 John 4:7–16

This is real love—not that we loved God, but that he loved us and sent his Son as a sacrifice to take away our sins.

1 John 4:10

Many people are their own worst enemies. "Well, I'm so overweight. I've blown my diet. I don't spend enough time with my children. I'm so undisciplined I didn't even clean my house last week. Surely, God is not pleased with me."

Don't step into that trap. Scripture indicates that God has already approved and accepted you. It doesn't say God approves you as long as you live a perfect life. No, it says God approves you unconditionally, just as you are. Frankly, it's not because of what you have or haven't done; God loves you because of who you are and because of who He is. God is love. You are a child of the Most High God. If God approves you, why don't you start approving yourself? Shake off guilt, condemnation, inadequacies, and a sense that you can't measure up, and start feeling good about who you are.

"Well, Joel, I don't know if I believe that," a dear, well-meaning man told me. "We're just poor old sinners."

No, we used to be poor old sinners, but when we came to Christ, He washed away our sins. He made us new creatures. Now, we are no longer poor old sinners, we are sons and daughters of the Most

High God. Instead of crawling around the floor with that "poor old me" mentality, you can step up to the dinner table. God has an incredible banquet prepared for you. He has an abundant life for you. No matter how many mistakes you've made in the past, or what sort of difficulties you struggle with right now, you have been destined to live in victory. You may not be all you want to be, but at least you can look back and say, "Thank You, God; I'm not what I used to be."

If God approves you, why don't you start approving yourself?

The Enemy doesn't want you to understand that you have been made righteous. He much prefers you to have a sin consciousness, but God wants you to have a righteousness consciousness. Start dwelling on the fact that you've been chosen, set apart, approved, and accepted in heaven—and that you have been made righteous on earth.

Every morning, no matter how we feel, we need to get out of bed and boldly declare, "Father, I thank You that You have approved me. Thank You that You are pleased with me. Thank You that I am forgiven. I know that I am Your friend."

Just as you put on your clothes, consciously put on the breastplate of God's approval. All through the day, everywhere you go, imagine big bold letters right across your chest saying Approved by Almighty God. When those condemning voices attempt to pummel your self-image with comments such as *You're not this, you're not that, you blew it over here,* simply look in the mirror and see that affirmation: Approved by Almighty God.

Today's Prayer to Become a Better You

Father, I thank You that You have approved me, that You are pleased with me. Thank You that I am forgiven. Thank You for calling me Your friend.

❧ Today's Thought to Become a Better You ❧

I am approved, accepted, and loved by Almighty God.

AGREEING WITH GOD

Once again you will have compassion on us. You will trample our sins under your feet and throw them into the depths of the ocean!

Micah 7:19

It's time for you to get in agreement with God and start feeling good about who you are. Certainly, you may have some areas in which you need to improve, and you will because you're growing. You're making progress. You can live free from the heaviness that has weighed you down in the past.

Keep in mind, it's the Enemy who accuses that you're never doing enough. *You're not working hard enough, not being a good enough marriage partner or parent; you did fairly well on your diet yesterday, but you shouldn't have eaten that dessert late last night.*

Don't take that stuff. You have a multitude of good qualities to every one negative quality.

"But, Joel, I'm so impatient."

Well, that may be true, but have you ever thought about the fact that you're always on time? You're persistent. You're determined.

"I don't think I'm as good a mom as I should be."

Maybe not, but have you noticed that your children are doing great in school? Your children never miss a meal. They are healthy, well rounded socially, and busy in sports, school, and church activities.

"Well, I'm not a very good husband, Joel."

Okay, maybe you work too much, but you've never missed a house payment. You provide a great living for your family.

"But I've made a lot of mistakes in life."

Get in agreement with God, and start feeling good about who you are.

Yes, but you picked up this book and began reading, learning, seeking to change for the better. That's a pretty great choice. Give yourself the benefit of the doubt. Take off those rags of condemnation, and start putting on your robe of righteousness. Put on the breastplate of God's approval.

You can, and you should, feel good about yourself. When you regard yourself positively, you are in agreement with God.

"What about that mistake I made last week? What about that time I failed last year?"

The moment you repented, God not only forgave you, He forgot about it. He chooses not to remember it anymore. Quit bringing up what God has already forgotten; let it go and start feeling good about who you are. We tend to think God is keeping a list of all our mistakes. In your mind, you can see Him up there in heaven. *Oops! They failed there, let me get that down.* And *Uh-oh, I heard that comment. Gabriel, make a special note of that one.*

That's not God's heart at all. God is for you; He is on your side. He is the best friend you could ever have. God is not looking at what you've done wrong; He's looking at what you've done right. He's not focused on what you are; He's focused on what you can become.

You can be assured that God is pleased with you. He's in the process of changing you. That's why I can get up every morning and, even though I make mistakes, boldly say, "God, I know you approve me, so I feel good about who I am."

❧ Today's Prayer to Become a Better You ❧

*It takes some getting used to the idea that You approve me,
Father. Thank You for freeing me to live for You rather than to
live afraid of You.*

❧ Today's Thought to Become a Better You ❧

*God isn't looking at what I've done wrong; He's looking at
what I've done right.*

THE POWER IN WORDS

SCRIPTURE READING TO BECOME A BETTER YOU   Proverbs 18:19–21

> *The tongue can bring death or life; those who love to talk*
> *will reap the consequences.*
>
> PROVERBS 18:21

GOD DIDN'T CREATE any of us to be average. He didn't make us to barely get by. We were created to excel. Scripture teaches that before the foundation of the world, God not only chose us, but He equipped us with everything we need to live His abundant life (see Ephesians 1:4–14). You have seeds of greatness inside of you, but it is up to you to believe and act on them.

I see too many people today going around with low self-esteem, feeling inferior, as if they don't have what it takes. As long as we have that poor self-image, we're not going to experience God's best. You will never rise above the image that you have of yourself. That's why it is so important that we see ourselves as God sees us.

You need to have an image of a champion on the inside. You may not be there yet; you may have some areas to overcome, but you need to know deep down inside that you are a victor and not a victim.

One of the best ways that we can improve our self-image is with our words. Words are like seeds. They have creative power. It says in Isaiah that "We will eat the fruit of our words." That's amazing when you stop to consider that truth: Our words tend to produce what we're saying.

Every day, we should make positive declarations over our lives. We should say things such as, "I am blessed. I am prosperous. I am healthy. I am talented. I am creative. I am wise." When we do that, we are building up our self-image. As those words permeate your heart and mind, and especially your subconscious mind, eventually they will begin to change the way you see your-self.

Our words set the direction for our lives.

Scripture says, "With our tongue, we can either bless our life or we can curse our life" (see James 3:10).

Some individuals curse their own futures by saying things such as, "I don't have what it takes. I'm so clumsy I can't get anything right. I'm so undisciplined. I'll probably never lose this weight."

We must be extremely careful what we allow out of our mouths. Our words set the direction for our lives.

Which direction are you going? Are you declaring good things? Are you blessing your life, speaking words of faith over your future and your children's future? Or are you prone to saying negative things? "Nothing good ever happens to me. I'll probably never get out of debt. I'll never break this addiction."

When you talk like that, you are setting the limits for your life.

Maybe you have had other people speak negative, destructive words over you. Perhaps a parent, coach, or teacher said things like, "You don't have what it takes, you're never going to be successful, you can't go to that college; you're not smart enough." Now those words have taken root and are setting the limits for your life. Unfortunately, you've heard those comments for so long they have seeped down into your self-image. The only way you can change the effects of those words is by going on the offensive and speaking faith-filled words over your life. Moreover, the best eraser you can ever find is God's Word. Start speaking out of your own mouth what God says about you: "I am anointed; I am approved; I am equipped; I've been chosen, set apart, destined to live in victory."

When you speak such faith-filled words, you will bless your life. Furthermore, your self-image will begin to improve.

⧜ Today's Prayer to Become a Better You ⧜

Father, help me each day to replace my words about myself with Your words about me. Thank You for the healing power of Your Word.

⧜ Today's Thought to Become a Better You ⧜

Today I will strive to keep my thoughts and words about myself consistent with what my heavenly Father says about me.

TALKING TOWARD A BETTER YOU

Scripture Reading to Become a Better You   Romans 4:16–25

Even when there was no reason for hope, Abraham kept hoping—believing that he would become the father of many nations. For God had said to him, "That's how many descendants you will have!"

ROMANS 4:18

POSITIVELY OR NEGATIVELY, creative power resides in your words, because you believe your words more than you believe anybody else's. Think about it. Your words go out of your mouth and come right back into your own ears. If you hear those comments long enough, they will drop down into your spirit, and those words will produce exactly what you're saying.

That's why it is so important that we get in a habit of declaring good things over our lives every day. When you get up in the morning, instead of looking at that mirror and saying, "Oh, I can't believe I look like this. I'm getting so old, so wrinkled," you need to smile and say, "Good morning, you good-looking thing!" No matter how you feel, look at yourself in that mirror and say, "I am strong. I am healthy. God is renewing my strength like the eagle's. And I am excited about this day."

In the natural, physical realm, those statements may not seem to be true. You may not feel up to par that day. Or you may have many obstacles to overcome. Scripture tells us that we are to "call the things that are not as if they already were" (see Romans 4:17).

In other words, don't talk about the way you are; talk about the way you want to be. That's what faith is all about. In the physical realm, you have to see it to believe it, but God says you have to believe it, and then you'll see it.

Change the way you speak about yourself, and you can change your life.

For instance, you may be undisciplined in a certain area, but instead of complaining about it and talking badly about yourself, start calling in what you need.

Change the way you speak about yourself, and you can change your life. Start each day saying things such as, "I am disciplined. I have self-control. I make good decisions. I'm an overcomer. This problem didn't come to stay; it came to pass." All through the day—as you're driving to work, taking a shower, or cooking dinner—under your breath, declare positive, biblically accurate statements about yourself: "I am more than a conqueror. I can do what I need to do. I'm a child of the Most High God."

As you speak affirmatively about yourself, you'll be amazed to discover that you are getting stronger emotionally and spiritually and that image on the inside is changing for the better.

Jacqueline is a bright young high-school student, but she did not believe she could ever make good grades. "I'm just a C student," she lamented. "That's the best I've ever done. I don't understand math. My teacher is the hardest one around."

Fortunately, Jacqueline learned to stop limiting herself by her words. Now each day on the way to school, she says, "I excel in school; I am a quick learner; I have good study habits; I am a good student; I am full of God's wisdom."

Maybe you tend to be critical and judgmental toward people. Don't sit back and say, "That's the way I am."

Instead, look in that mirror and say, "I am compassionate; I am kind; I am sympathetic and understanding; I believe the best in people." As you consistently make these positive declarations, the new attitudes will get down inside you, and your relationships will begin to change.

⚛ Today's Prayer to Become a Better You ⚛

Father, I realize I'm exercising faith when I put into words the way You see me. Help me to live out Your plans for me.

⚛ Today's Thought to Become a Better You ⚛

God keeps improving the good work He is doing in me!

SPEAKING INTO YOUR FUTURE

SCRIPTURE READING TO BECOME A BETTER YOU   Habakkuk 2:1–4

The LORD said to me, "Write my answer plainly on tablets, so that a runner can carry the correct message to others."

HABAKKUK 2:2

WITH OUR WORDS, we can prophesy our own futures. Unfortunately, many people predict defeat, failure, lack, and mediocrity. Avoid those kinds of comments, and use your words to declare good things. Declare health, joy, financial blessing, happy and whole relationships. All through the day, you can declare, "I have the favor of God. I can do what I need to do." As you do so, you will be blessing your own life and strengthening your self-image.

If you struggle with depression, use your words to change your situation. You may have been through a lot of disappointments. You may have gone through some setbacks in the past. More than anybody, you need to get up every day and boldly declare, "This is going to be a great day. I may have been defeated in the past, but this is a new day. God is on my side. Things are changing in my favor."

When discouraging thoughts attack, instead of complaining and expecting the worst, say it again and again: "Something good is going to happen to me. I'm a victor and not a victim." It's not enough to merely think positively: You need to speak positively about yourself. You need to hear it over and over again. "Good things are coming my way. God is fighting my battles for me. New doors of opportunity are opening."

As you speak affirmatively, you will develop a new image on the inside, and things will begin to change in your favor.

If you will set aside five minutes a day and simply declare good things over your life, you may be astounded at the results. Before you start your busy day, before you leave the house, drive to work, or take the kids to school, take a few minutes to speak blessings

Something supernatural happens when we speak it out.

over your life. You may prefer to write the statements so you can have a record of them. It says in Habakkuk to write down your vision. Make a list of your dreams, goals, and aspirations as well as the areas you want to improve, the things you want to see changed. Always make sure you can back it all up with God's Word. Then get alone with God, and take a few minutes every day to declare good things over your life. Remember, it's not enough to read it or merely think about it. Something supernatural happens when we speak it out. That's how we give life to our faith.

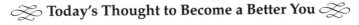

✎ Today's Prayer to Become a Better You ✎

Father, let me declare out loud that this is going to be a great day. I may have been defeated in the past, but this is a new day. You are on my side. Things are changing in my favor.

✎ Today's Thought to Become a Better You ✎

What I want to be I need to see and say.

THINKING RIGHT

Scripture Reading to Become a Better You · Psalm 42:1–11

Why am I discouraged? Why is my heart so sad? I will put my hope in God! I will praise him again—my Savior and my God!

PSALM 42:11

Each of us has an internal dialogue, an inner conversation going on with ourselves throughout the day. In fact, we talk more to ourselves than we do to anybody else. The question is, What are you saying to yourself? What do you meditate on? Positive thoughts? Empowering thoughts? Affirming thoughts? Or do you go around thinking negative, defeated thoughts, telling yourself things like *I'm unattractive. I'm not talented. I've made too many mistakes. I'm sure God is displeased with me.* That kind of negative self-talk keeps millions of people from rising higher.

We usually talk to ourselves subconsciously without even thinking about it. But in the back of your mind, you have these reoccurring thoughts. And for most people those thoughts are negative: *I'm clumsy. I'll never overcome my past. I don't have what it takes.*

All through the day they allow defeatist messages to permeate their minds and self-talk. They see somebody who's successful, somebody who's achieving, and that inner voice tells them, *That will never happen for me. I'm not as smart as that person; I'm not that talented.* Or they see somebody who is in good physical shape, somebody who looks healthy, fit, and attractive. That voice tells them, *I'm just not that disciplined. I'll never get back in shape.* There's a negative voice on the inside that's constantly telling the person that something is wrong with them.

You're not a good mother. You didn't work hard enough last week. You are a weak person. If we make the mistake of allowing this negative self-talk to take root, it not only saddens our spirits, but it also limits how high we can go in life. Many people are living in mediocrity because they are playing that negative recording day after day, over and over again.

We talk more to ourselves than we do to anybody else.

I've discovered that often these wrong-thinking patterns stem from childhood. The people who should have been nurturing us and telling us what we could become, building our confidence, did just the opposite. I know people who are stuck in ruts because as they were growing up, somebody mistreated them, or somebody rejected them. A parent, a coach, or even a peer spoke negative words over the person. They didn't know any better. They just let it take root. Now those wrong-thinking patterns are keeping them from becoming all God intends them to be.

We have to reprogram our minds. Please don't lie in bed every morning, thinking about everything that's wrong with you. Don't rehearse all your mistakes—thinking about what you can't do or how you don't have what it takes. It doesn't matter how many times you've tried and failed. Shake off those negative messages and experiences and put on a new recording. Remind yourself often: *I am a child of the Most High God. I have a bright future. God is pleased with me. I am talented; I am creative; I have what it takes. I will fulfill my destiny.* We should be talking to ourselves that way, not in arrogance but in quiet confidence. Deep down on the inside, all through the day, we should hear things like *I am anointed. I am called. I am chosen. I am equipped. This is my season.*

∾ **Today's Prayer to Become a Better You** ∾

Father, remind me of the example in today's Psalm. I choose to see discouragement as a reminder to renew my trust and hope in You.

∾ **Today's Thought to Become a Better You** ∾

God has given me all I need to live for Him.

CHANGE THE CHANNEL

SCRIPTURE READING TO BECOME A BETTER YOU   Psalm 46:1–10

Be still, and know that I am God!

PSALM 46:10

PAY ATTENTION TO how you talk to yourself. If you will talk to yourself in the right way, you'll not only enjoy your life more, but you'll rise higher to a new level of confidence, a new level of boldness. I read a study where researchers gave a group of college students special eyeglasses that turned everything upside down, totally opposite of what it should be. For the first few days of the experiment, confusion reigned. The students stumbled over the furniture, they couldn't read or write, they had to be led to class, and they could barely function. But slowly, they started adjusting.

By the end of the first week, they were able to go to class on their own. They didn't need any help to get around. The researchers were intrigued, so they decided to continue the experiment. After one month, the students had totally adapted. Their minds had compensated for their upside-down world, and they could read without any problem. They could write, do their homework, type on the computer—all upside down.

Something similar can happen to us. If we go around with wrong mind-sets long enough, telling ourselves, *Well, I'm not a good parent. I've made too many mistakes. Nothing good ever happens to me,* just like those college students, even though it's totally backward, and not the way God created us, our minds will eventually adapt and adjust, and we will end up living at that level.

Your world may be upside down already. Maybe you are living far below your potential, feeling bad about yourself, lacking confidence, and wallowing in low self-esteem. Have you considered that it could be a result of what you are constantly speaking to yourself? Your internal dialogue is negative. You have to change that before anything else will change.

You have to change on the inside before change will happen on the outside.

Don't listen to voices that are pulling you down, even if they are your own voice. You may not look like you stepped out of a fashion magazine, but I can tell you this: You were made in the image of Almighty God. You will be amazed at how much more you enjoy your life and how much better you feel about yourself if you'll learn to talk to yourself in a positive manner. And even when you make mistakes, even when you do wrong, don't go around saying, "Well, I can't do anything right. I'm so clumsy. I'm so slow."

Learn to put on that new recording, tell yourself "I am forgiven. I am restored. God has a new plan. Good things are in store."

I'm not saying simply to take the easy way out. I am saying that it does you no good to go around feeling condemned, disgraced, or disqualified over something that is in the past. I know people who live with a black cloud following them around. It's a vague feeling; they can't even put their finger on it, but something is always telling them, *You're never going to be happy. You might as well forget it.*

You cannot sit back and accept those kinds of statements about yourself. You must rise up and start talking to yourself in a new way. All through the day, you should be telling yourself things like, "Something good is going to happen to me. God is pleased with me. I have a bright future. The best is yet to come." You have to change on the inside before change will happen on the outside.

✖ Today's Prayer to Become a Better You ✖

Father, I want to talk to You more often, and I want to talk more truthfully about myself. Help me talk about me the way You think about me.

✖ Today's Thought to Become a Better You ✖

I will echo God's wonderful words about me over and over again.

GREAT EXPECTATIONS

The LORD said to Joshua, "Today I have rolled away the shame of your slavery in Egypt." So that place has been called Gilgal to this day.

JOSHUA 5:9

GOD TOLD THE CHILDREN of Israel in Joshua 5, verse 9, "This day have I rolled away the reproach of Egypt from you." In other words, they didn't feel good about themselves. They had been hurt and mistreated; they were discouraged, even after being delivered from slavery. God came to them and said, "Stop doing that. I am rolling away the reproach from you." I believe the reproach had to be rolled away before they could go into the Promised Land.

It's the same with us. You may be trying to live in victory, trying to be successful, trying to have a good marriage. But you are negative toward yourself. You don't feel good about who you are. You're constantly dwelling on your past hurts and pains. Until you are willing to let go of those offenses and start focusing on your new possibilities, they will tie you down right where you are. You cannot have a bad attitude toward yourself and expect to have God's best. Quit focusing on what you've done wrong. God has already rolled away your reproach—your shame, embarrassment, failures, and setbacks.

God has done His part. Now you must do your part. Let it go so you can go into your Promised Land. Start thinking, feeling, and speaking positively about yourself.

Scripture says, "Our faith is made effectual when we acknowledge everything good in us" (see Philemon 1:6). Think about this: Our faith is not effective when we acknowledge all our hurts and pains. It's not effective when we stay focused on our shortcomings or our weaknesses. Our faith is most effective when we acknowledge the good things that are in us. Declare affirmations such as "I have a bright future. I am gifted. I am talented. People like me. I have the favor of God."

> Our faith
> is most effective
> when we acknowledge
> the good things
> that are in us.

When we believe in God's Son, Jesus Christ, and believe in ourselves, that's when our faith comes alive. When we believe we have what it takes, we focus on our possibilities.

Unfortunately, most people do just the opposite. They acknowledge everything wrong with them. Even subconsciously, they are constantly playing that negative recording, causing them to have a low opinion of themselves. If you are in that group, you must change that recording.

I may be *naive,* but I expect people to like me. I expect people to be friendly to me. I expect people to want to help me. I have a positive opinion about who I am because I know whose I am—I belong to Almighty God.

Don't walk into a room timid and insecure, thinking, *Nobody's going to like me in here. Look at them; they're probably talking about me already. I knew I shouldn't have worn this suit. I knew I should have stayed at home.*

No, get your inner dialogue going in a different direction. Develop a habit of being positive toward yourself; have a good opinion about who you are. "Well, Joel, I'm just a housewife. I'm just a businessperson. I'm just a schoolteacher."

No, you are not "just" anything. You are a child of the Most High God. You are fulfilling your purpose. The Lord orders your steps. Goodness and mercy are following you. You are a person of destiny.

You are not "just" anything.

Knowing and acknowledging these things can boost your confidence sky high.

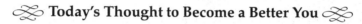 **Today's Prayer to Become a Better You**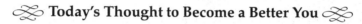

Father, thank You for making me someone You want to be with and through whom You want to work in the world. I'm available!

Today's Thought to Become a Better You

God's doing good things in me and through me today.

PART THREE

DEVELOP BETTER RELATIONSHIPS

MAKING ANOTHER'S LIFE BETTER

SCRIPTURE READING TO BECOME A BETTER YOU 1 Corinthians 13:1–7

Love is patient and kind. Love is not jealous or boastful or proud.

1 CORINTHIANS 13:4

IF YOU WANT your life to increase, if you want your life to get better, then you need to help improve somebody else's life. If you will help somebody else become successful, God will make sure that you are successful.

God puts people in our lives on purpose so we can help them succeed and help them become all He created them to be. Most people will not reach their full potential without somebody else believing in them. That means you and I have an assignment. Everywhere we go, we should be encouraging people, building them up, challenging them to reach for new heights. When people are around us, they should leave better off than they were previously. Rather than feeling discouraged or defeated, people should feel challenged and inspired after spending any time with you and me.

The Bible says that love is kind. One translation says, "Love looks for a way of being constructive." In other words, love looks for ways to help improve somebody else's life. Take time to make a difference. Don't just obsess about how you can make your own life better. Think about how you can make somebody else's life better as well. Our attitude should be, "Who can I encourage today? Who can I build up? How can I improve somebody else's life?"

You have something to offer that nobody else can give. Somebody needs your encouragement. Somebody needs to know that you believe in him, that you're for her, that you think he or she has what it takes to succeed. If you look back over your own life, most likely you'll find someone who played a pivotal role in helping you get to where you are today. Maybe your parents or a teacher had confidence in you and helped you believe in yourself. Perhaps it was a boss who placed you in a higher position even though you didn't feel qualified at the time. Or a school counselor who said, "You've got what it takes. You can go to this college. You can be successful in that career."

You have something to offer that nobody else can give.

Maybe they saw something in you that you may not have seen in yourself, and they helped you get to that next level. Now, it's your turn to do something similar for somebody else. Who are you believing in? Who are you cheering on? Who are you helping to become successful? Friend, there's no greater investment in life than in being a people builder. Relationships are more important than our accomplishments.

Today's Prayer to Become a Better You

Father, You have shown me love by Your kindness to me. Help me see ways I can pass on that kindness to others today and make their lives better.

Today's Thought to Become a Better You

I'm delivering kindness and love into someone's life today.

BELIEVING THE BEST

SCRIPTURE READING TO BECOME A BETTER YOU   1 Corinthians 8:1–6

While knowledge makes us feel important, it is love that strengthens the church.

1 CORINTHIANS 8:1

YOU HAVE THINGS on the inside of you—gifts and talents—that you've not yet dreamed of using. You can go further and accomplish more. Don't settle for the status quo. You can overcome any challenge that's before you. You can break any addiction. You have the power of the Most High God on the inside of you.

The Bible says in 1 Corinthians 8:1, that love encourages people to grow to their full stature. When you believe the best in people, you help to bring the best out of them. Many people simply need somebody to spark a bit of hope, somebody to say, "Yes, you can do it. You've got what it takes."

Are you believing the best in your own children? Are you instilling the confidence in them that they need, telling them that they're going to do great things in life? Are you believing the best in your loved ones? Maybe some of them have gotten off course. Don't give up on them; don't write them off. Make sure they know that you're concerned. Make sure they know that you really believe in them.

Here's the key: Don't focus on what they are right now. Focus on what they can become. See the potential on the inside. They may have some bad habits, or they may be doing some things that you don't like, but don't judge them for it. Don't look down on them critically. Find some way to challenge them to rise higher. Tell them, "I'm praying for you. I believe you're going to break that addiction. I'm believing for great things in your life."

When you believe the best in people, you help to bring the best out of them.

You'll be pleasantly surprised at how people respond when they know you really care. Everywhere Jesus went, He saw potential in people that they didn't see in themselves. He didn't focus on their weaknesses or their faults. He saw them the way they could become.

Today's Prayer to Become a Better You

Help me today, Father, to see the best and speak the best into other people's lives. Let me do for them some of what You have done for me.

Today's Thought to Become a Better You

I can help bring the best out of someone today.

WHAT MATTERS MOST

Scripture Reading to Become a Better You   James 5:7–11

Don't grumble about each other, brothers and sisters, or you will be judged. For look—the Judge is standing at the door!

JAMES 5:9

To maintain healthy relationships, we need to learn how to keep the strife out of our lives. God made each of us as a unique individual. We have different personalities and temperaments; we approach issues in different ways, so we really shouldn't be surprised when we grate against one another occasionally. Too often, though, if someone doesn't agree with our opinion, or see eye to eye with us on some matter, we get bent out of shape and allow strife to foment. I've discovered that just because somebody is not exactly like me or doesn't do things the way I do them doesn't necessarily mean I am right and the other person is wrong. We're just different, and our differences can cause friction.

It takes maturity to get along with somebody who is different from you. It takes patience not to start a dispute over minor issues or become easily offended. If we're going to keep the strife out of our lives, then we must learn how to give people the benefit of the doubt.

We will also need to overlook some things. Every person has faults; we all have weaknesses. We should not expect the people with whom we are in relationships to be perfect. No matter how great someone may be, no matter how much you love him or her, if you are around that person long enough, you will have an opportunity to be offended. There is no such thing as a perfect spouse, a perfect boss, or even a perfect pastor (although I'm very close!).

We really shouldn't be surprised when we grate against one another occasionally.

If we're putting unrealistic expectations on people, expecting them to be perfect, that is not fair to them, and it will be a source of frustration for us. We're always going to be disappointed.

Some people live with the attitude, "I'll love you as long as you never hurt me or as long as you never make a mistake. I'll be your friend as long as you treat me just right. As long as you do things my way, then I'll accept you, and I'll be happy."

But that is extremely unfair and places too much pressure on that other person. Scripture teaches that love makes allowances for people's weaknesses. Love covers a person's faults. In other words, you have to overlook some things. Quit demanding perfection out of your spouse, your children, or other people with whom you are in a relationship, and learn to show a little mercy.

I couldn't find a better wife than Victoria. She is an extremely loving, caring, generous person, and yet there are some things I have to overlook, some things for which I have to make allowances. That doesn't mean something is wrong with her; she's just human. If I were a critical faultfinder, keeping an account of everything she did wrong, then our relationship would suffer. Before long, we'd be at odds with each other, arguing, and fighting.

Instead, we make allowances for each other's weaknesses. We've learned not to wear our feelings on our sleeves and not to be easily offended.

Few things are worse than living with a touchy, overly sensitive person. If somebody offends you or does you wrong, learn to shake it off and move on. Scripture teaches that love believes the best in people.

"Well, my husband hardly spoke to me this morning. He didn't even thank me for cooking dinner the other night," a wife might say.

Remember, love covers a fault. Instead of going through the day offended and upset, consider the fact that he may not have been feeling up to par. Maybe he's under a lot of pressure at work or stressed out over some other matter. Rather than criticizing and condemning, give him the benefit of the doubt and believe the best in him.

❧ Today's Prayer to Become a Better You ❧

Father, thank You for the special people in my life. Remind me to forgive them as You forgive me. Help me see them as You see them!

❧ Today's Thought to Become a Better You ❧

The heavier the offense, the less it's worth carrying.

LEARNING TO MAKE PEACE

SCRIPTURE READING TO BECOME A BETTER YOU   Mark 3:20–27

A family splintered by feuding will fall apart.

MARK 3:25

THE BIBLE TEACHES, "We need to adapt and adjust in order to keep the peace" (see Romans 12:16). It doesn't say that other people should adapt and adjust to us. No, if we are going to have peace, we have to be willing to change.

You can't have this attitude: "Well, if my wife would start doing what I ask her, then we'd have peace. If my husband will start picking up his stuff, then we'll get along fine. If my boss would start treating me right, then I'd quit being so rude to him."

I know people who have gotten a divorce all because they stayed stirred up over something silly or ultimately insignificant. They allowed the sore to fester, and before long they were lunging at each other's throats. Deep down inside, they may really love each other, but through the years, they've allowed strife to drive a wedge into their relationship.

Jesus said, "A house divided is continually being brought to destruction and it will not stand." Notice, if you allow strife into your relationship, that relationship will be brought to destruction. It may not happen overnight; it might not happen in a couple of months or even a few years. If you allow strife to grow by holding grudges, making sarcastic remarks, or otherwise, you may not realize it, but that relationship is in the process of being destroyed.

Strife is chipping away at your foundation, and unless you decide to do something about it soon, your life could crumble into a mess. You could very well look up one day and think, *What have I done? I've destroyed this relationship. How could I have been so foolish?*

Don't be hardheaded and stubborn. Maybe you have been at odds with somebody for months, not speaking to them, giving them the cold shoulder. Life is too short to live it that way. If possible, go to that person and make things right—while you still have the opportunity.

**It's not always about being right.
It's about keeping strife out of your life.**

I recently spoke with a man who was broken and defeated. When I asked him what was troubling him, he explained how he and his father got at odds with each other over a business decision. They hadn't spoken in over two years. He said, "Joel, I knew deep down inside that I needed to make it right, but I kept putting it off. Then earlier this week, I received a call informing me that my father had suffered a heart attack and died." Imagine what emotional pain that man is living with.

Don't wait until you cannot make amends with someone from whom you are estranged. Do it today; swallow your pride, and apologize even if it wasn't your fault. Keep the peace. Understand, it's not always about being right. It's about keeping strife out of your life. You can win every argument, but if it opens the door to turmoil, brings division, and tears you apart, in the end you didn't win at all—and you may have lost a lot.

I believe that God always gives us a warning, a wake-up call of sorts. He may say simply, *Stop being so argumentative. Quit being a faultfinder. Quit keeping your record books. Start being a peace-maker.* When we recognize His voice, we need to respond.

"But I apologized first last time. That's not fair. It's his turn to apologize."

It may not be fair, but it can keep you together. Swallow your pride. Be the bigger person. When you do that, you are sowing a seed of love and kindness, and God will always make it up to you.

⤜ Today's Prayer to Become a Better You ⤛

As much as it is up to me, Father, I want to live at peace in our home. Please heal divisions and make me a peacemaker.

⤜ Today's Thought to Become a Better You ⤛

Today I will live as an instrument of God's peace.

PROTECT YOUR FAMILY

SCRIPTURE READING TO BECOME A BETTER YOU   Nehemiah 4:1–23

*As I looked over the situation, I called together the nobles
and the rest of the people and said to them, "Don't be
afraid of the enemy! Remember the Lord, who is great
and glorious, and fight for your brothers, your sons, your
daughters, your wives, and your homes!"*

NEHEMIAH 4:14

ONE OF THE GREATEST THREATS we face in the twenty-first century
is not a terrorist attack or an ecological catastrophe, but an attack on
our homes. The Enemy would love nothing more than to ruin your
relationship with your husband or wife, your parents, or your children. Too many homes are being destroyed through strife, lack of
commitment, wrong priorities, and bad attitudes. If we're going to
have strong, healthy relationships, we must dig our heels in and fight
for our families.

The Old Testament records a time when Nehemiah was rebuilding
the walls of Jerusalem. The walls had been torn down years previously, and the enemy was coming against God's people, against their
homes, their wives and children, while the men worked on the con-
struction crews. The situation got so bad that Nehemiah instructed
his men to work with a hammer in one hand and a sword in the
other. He encouraged them, "Men, fight for your sons, fight for your
daughters, fight for your wives, fight for your families" (see Nehemiah
4:14). He went on to say, "If you will fight, then God will fight."

I believe God is saying something similar to us today. If we will do our part and take a strong stand for our families, God will do His part. He'll help us to have great marriages and great relationships with our parents and children.

If you will fight, then God will fight!

Certainly, not everyone will get married, but if a man and a woman choose to marry, two issues must be settled first. Number one: As a couple, we are committed to God. We're going to live a life that honors Him. We will be people of excellence and integrity in all that we do.

The second settled issue must be that as a couple, we are committed to each other. Occasionally, we may disagree, say things we shouldn't; we might even pout or get downright angry. But when it's all said and done, we're going to get over it, and we will forgive and move on. Leaving is not an option. We're committed to each other through the good times and the tough times.

If bailing out of the relationship is an option or an alternative, then you will always find some reason to justify it. "Joel, we just can't get along. We're not compatible. We tried, but we just don't love each other anymore."

Truth is, no two people are completely compatible. We have to learn to become so. That means we may have to make sacrifices; we may have to overlook some things. We must be willing to compromise for the good of the relationship.

The perfect spouse does not exist. Victoria sometimes tells people, "Oh, my husband, Joel, is the perfect husband."

Don't believe that for a minute. She is saying that by faith!

Stick with your spouse and make that relationship work. As one lady quipped, "My husband and I got married for better or for worse. He couldn't do any better and I couldn't do any worse."

When you do have disagreements, learn to disagree from the neck up. Don't let it get down in your heart. Victoria and I don't always see eye to eye, but we've learned how to agree to disagree.

When you present your case, don't try to make that other person change his or her mind. Give others the right to have their own opinions. If you're not going to be happy unless they agree with you, then really you're simply trying to manipulate them. You're trying to force your opinion on them. The better approach is to present your case, share your heart, and then step back and allow God to work in that person or situation.

✷ Today's Prayer to Become a Better You ✷

Father, keep me from selfishness, and help me fight for my family. We can definitely use the help You have promised. I welcome You in our home.

✷ Today's Thought to Become a Better You ✷

I'm committed to seeing my family become a better family.

WHEN FIGHTING MEANS LOVING

Her children stand and bless her. Her husband praises her.
PROVERBS 31:28

IF WE ARE GOING to be successful in standing up and fighting *for* our families we will have to constantly work on the quality of love and encouragement *in* our families. Because the writer of Proverbs 31 praised his wife, his children rose up and blessed her as well. Unquestionably, when a husband praises and blesses his wife, their children will follow his example.

How a man treats his wife will have a profound impact on how his children will respect and honor their mother. Your children subconsciously take in voice tones, body language, and personal demeanor.

And Dad, your daughter will most likely marry somebody much like you. If you are hard-nosed and disrespectful, speaking rude, hurtful things to your spouse, don't be surprised if your daughter gravitates toward somebody with those same characteristics. I realize I need to treat my wife the way I want somebody to treat my daughter.

And Mom, you need to treat your husband the way you want somebody to treat your sons.

Men, open the car door for your wife. Take her coffee in the morning. Go out of your way to show her love, honor, and respect. I heard somebody say, "If a man ever opens the car door for his wife, he's either got a new car or a new wife." Perhaps we need to return to a society that encourages men to respect and honor women.

"If I do that sort of thing, my friends may think I'm a weakling," a guy might say. "They may give me a hard time."

If that's the case, you probably ought to find some new friends. A real man's masculinity is not diminished because he opens the car door for his wife. Being male doesn't necessarily make you a man. Treating people with dignity and respect makes you a man. Taking care of your wife and family makes you a man. Watching over your children makes you a man. Speaking blessings over your wife and kids—that's being a real man.

Granted,
you may not have
grown up in that
kind of loving
environment,
but you can set
a new standard.

Granted, you may not have grown up in that kind of loving environment, but you can set a new standard. You can raise the bar.

In the human reproduction process, the father provides the child's gender. The female egg contributes two X chromosomes; the male sperm contributes an X or a Y chromosome. If the father gives the egg an X, the baby will be a girl. If he gives a Y, the baby will be a boy. So, fathers, you have the ultimate influence over your children's gender.

Fathers, you have incredible influence over them in other ways as well. You need to make especially sure that you affirm your children. Every day, just as you bless your wife, bless your children as well. Look at each child and say, "I'm so proud of you. I think you're great. There's nothing you can't do." Your children need your approval. You're helping them to form their identity. If, as fathers, we're too busy, we're never there, or maybe we're just always correcting our children without providing them with affirmation, our children are not going to be as confident and secure as they should be.

Certainly, there are times when the father can't be there for his children because of other responsibilities. Nonetheless, do your best to keep your priorities in order. No amount of success in your career can make up for failure at home. I've seen some men accomplish great things in the corporate world as business leaders but at the expense of their children. Their children grew up without a father figure.

Fathers, take your children to church; don't send them. Be at their ball games as often as possible. Know who their friends are. Listen to their music. Children are looking for direction and guidance. When that young man comes over to take your daughter out on a date, be the first one at the door. Let him know there's a man in the house watching over that young lady. Parents, we have to fight for our children.

If we will fight for them, God will fight with us.

 Today's Prayer to Become a Better You

Father, help me bless my family. Help me speak and deliver good into their lives. I want to be the kind of family member You designed me to be.

Today's Thought to Become a Better You

I'm fighting for my family when I bless them today.

WHAT CHILDREN NEED

SCRIPTURE READING TO BECOME A BETTER YOU   Deuteronomy 6:1–9

You must commit yourselves wholeheartedly to these commands that I am giving you today. Repeat them again and again to your children. Talk about them when you are at home and when you are on the road, when you are going to bed and when you are getting up.

DEUTERONOMY 6:6–7

Y EARS AGO, the largest game reserve in South Africa developed an overpopulation of elephants. The curators decided to take three hundred of the youngest male elephants and separate them from their parents and other adult elephants. The "orphans" were transported to another national park, where the white rhinoceros reigned as the dominant "king of the park." The rhinoceros has no natural enemies. Nothing stalks it, not even a lion, a tiger, or a bear.

The rhino is simply too powerful. As such, the curators felt there would be no problem mixing the orphan elephants in with the rhinos. Over time, however, they began to find dead rhinos out in the brush. They couldn't understand what was happening, so they set up surveillance cameras to observe the park. Much to their surprise, they found that those young male elephants, the ones that no longer had a father or mother figure, had formed gangs and had viciously attacked the rhino population. It's not even in the elephant's God-given natural instincts to act that way, but the lack of parental influence spawned the strange, deadly phenomenon.

I believe a similar plight threatens our children. The reason that children get in trouble can often be traced to the fact that they do not have positive role models in their lives. They don't have anybody speaking blessings over them and praying for them; they don't have father figures, and many don't have healthy, positive mother figures.

Stand up for your family and then be "family" to someone else.

It doesn't mean these children are incorrigible; it is simply a fact that without parental guidance, children sometimes do things they might not otherwise do if Mom or Dad were around.

We have a responsibility to reach out to children who don't have a father figure or a mother figure. Maybe you can mentor a young man or a young woman. If you really want to be blessed, don't just fight for your family, fight for somebody else's family. Stand in the gap for that single mom or single dad. When you take your son out to hit baseballs, swing by and pick up that young man who doesn't have a father figure. Reach out to some other children. Help them discover their identity.

Mandy grew up in a dysfunctional home. Her father was never around, and her mother had plenty of problems of her own. As a teenager, Mandy raised her younger brother. To all observers, it appeared that Mandy was handling the situation reasonably well, but on the inside, she was crying out for help.

One day a friend of hers at school mentioned that her father owned a fast-food restaurant. "Come on down, Mandy. Maybe my dad will give you a job," her friend suggested. Mandy visited the restaurant, and that gentleman not only gave her a job, but he also took her under his wing. He began to watch after her, making sure she changed the oil in her car, checking to see that she was doing okay in school, and on and on. He didn't even realize it, but he became the father figure for which Mandy longed. Years later, when

Mandy was about to get married, her real father was nowhere to be found. Can you guess who gave Mandy away at her wedding?

That's right; it was the man from the fast-food restaurant. He made time to care. He fought not only for his own family; he fought for somebody else's child too. Today, Mandy is healthy, whole, and happily married, much to the credit of a man who became a father figure to her. Stand up for your family and then be "family" to someone else who needs a father, mother, sister, or brother. As you take time for others, God will provide for you.

❧ Today's Prayer to Become a Better You ❧

Father, every time I talk to You, I'm using family language. Without family, I wouldn't be here. Thank You for making me part of Your family. Let me be a source of encouragement to those inside and close by my earthly family.

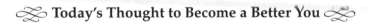

❧ Today's Thought to Become a Better You ❧

I can give the gift of family to someone today.

INVEST IN YOUR RELATIONSHIPS

The Hittites replied to Abraham, "Listen, my lord, you are an honored prince among us. Choose the finest of our tombs and bury her there. No one here will refuse to help you in this way."

Genesis 23:5–6

If you want your relationships to thrive, you must invest in them by being a giver rather than a taker. Everywhere you go, strive to make relational deposits into people's lives, encouraging them, building them up, and helping them to feel better about themselves.

Granted, it's not always easy. Some people are difficult to be around, because they tend to draw the life and energy out of you. They're not bad people; they just drain you. They always have a problem, or some major crisis that they are convinced requires your help to solve. They talk all the time, so much so that you can't get a word in edgewise. By the time the conversation is done, you feel as though your emotional energy is gone. Difficult people don't make positive deposits; they are too busy making withdrawals.

Please don't misunderstand. It's okay to be down and discouraged occasionally. Everybody has a right to have a bad day. But if you're like that all the time, that's a problem. You're not going to have good friendships if you're always draining the emotional reserves of the people around you.

I like to think of my relationships as "emotional bank accounts."

I have an account with every person with whom I have a relationship—whether a family member, a business associate, friends, even some of the people I meet in passing; I have an emotional account with the security guard at work, the man at the gas station, and the waiter at the restaurant. Every time I interact with them, I'm either making a deposit or making a withdrawal from their accounts.

Difficult people don't make positive deposits; they are too busy making withdrawals.

How do you make a deposit? It can be something as simple as taking the time to walk over and shake that man's hand. "How are you doing today? Good morning. Good to see you."

Just the simple fact that you went out of your way to make him feel important made a deposit into that account. Your act of kindness built trust and respect. You can make a deposit simply by smiling at people, acknowledging them, being friendly, being pleasant to them in ordinary circumstances.

When you compliment people, you're making a deposit. Tell that coworker, "That was an outstanding presentation. You did a great job." Tell your husband, "I appreciate what you do for this family." Tell your wife, "You make it so much fun to live around here." When you do such things, you are not merely giving a compliment, you are making a deposit into the account you share with that person.

At home, you can make deposits in your emotional bank accounts by giving your wife a hug and a kiss, telling her that you love her. You make deposits into your accounts with your children by spending time with them, by listening to your daughter when she's playing the piano, by going down to the park and watching your son skateboard.

A subtle yet amazingly effective means of making a deposit is by overlooking a fault. Maybe a coworker is rude to you and jumps down your throat about some meaningless matter. Instead of retaliating, you let it go. The next day when he apologizes, you say, "Don't even worry. I've already forgiven you. I didn't think twice about it. I knew that wasn't your normal self."

When you do such things, you make huge deposits into your account with that person. Your stock goes up significantly on his scale. Perhaps one day when you're a bit stressed and on edge, and maybe you don't treat him as well as you normally would, you'll have plenty in your account to cover it.

✑ Today's Prayer to Become a Better You ✑

Father, show me places in my life where I tend to be more of a taker than a giver. And then help me turn that around. I know I can make greater investments in the people in my life.

✑ Today's Thought to Become a Better You ✑

I'm going to make a generous deposit in someone's life today.

DEPOSIT FIRST

SCRIPTURE READING TO BECOME A BETTER YOU   Ephesians 4:29–32

*Let everything you say be good and helpful, so that your
words will be an encouragement to those who hear them.*
EPHESIANS 4:29

I T'S AMAZING how people will respond when they know that you're
rooting for them, that you are in their corner, wanting them to do
well. Oftentimes, they will be willing to change when they know
you're not trying to condemn them, that you are not trying to put
them down or make them feel bad about themselves. True correction
always inspires people to want to do better.

If you'll make it a priority to keep your emotional accounts full in
your relationships, you will have far fewer problems with people
receiving suggestions and receiving correction from you. In fact, one
expert says the first thirty seconds of a conversation will determine
the next hour. So when you have something sensitive to talk about,
when you have something that has potential to cause conflict or
problems, always start positively. Make sure it is the right time to
broach that matter. Make sure that you've thought about how
you're going to start the conversation, and be aware of your tone of
voice. Watch your body language. Keep a pleasant expression, and
choose to discuss the matter in love.

When you are trying to improve a relationship, if your words or
actions cause the other person to become defensive, you've defeated
your purpose. That person is not going to receive what you have to

say. She may get her feelings hurt, or he'll start pointing out your faults. "Well, who are you to tell me that?" he or she may retort.

"You're no better than I am! Do you think you're perfect?" If you approach matters in a better way, all that turmoil can be avoided.

The first thirty seconds of a conversation will determine the next hour.

Studies show that it takes five positive charges to override one negative charge. In other words, before you correct someone, make sure you have already given that person five compliments. Sadly, the correction-to-compliment ratio is nearly opposite that in our society today. We hear five things we're doing wrong to every one thing we're doing right. No wonder our relationships are not what they should be! Our accounts are overdrawn.

When we correct people, we should never belittle them or make them feel insignificant. At the office, don't have the attitude, "How could you come up with that? Whose lousy idea was this?" Instead, do your best to find the good in every suggestion, even if you can't use it.

It takes five positive charges to override one negative charge.

Remember, genuine love overlooks a fault. Love makes allowances for mistakes. True love sees the best in every person. If you want to make a huge deposit into somebody's life, when he makes a mistake and he knows he is wrong, don't make a big deal about it.

Don't embarrass a child in front of other family members or friends. Don't embarrass an employee in front of his or her coworkers. If you must confront someone about a matter, deal with him or her in private if at all possible, and always do your best to protect the person's dignity.

✌ Today's Prayer to Become a Better You ✌

Father, please bring to my mind (or bring across my path) those people into whose lives I can make a meaningful deposit today. And give me the gentle, encouraging words to speak.

✌ Today's Thought to Become a Better You ✌

I have the privilege of making priceless deposits in the lives of others today.

RANDOM DEPOSITS

SCRIPTURE READING TO BECOME A BETTER YOU   Philippians 2:1–4

Don't look out only for your own interests, but take an interest in others, too.

PHILIPPIANS 2:4

DON'T MAKE THE MISTAKE of living your life self-centered, rushing through your days concerned only about yourself. Take time for people; make them feel special; learn to appreciate them. When you see your mailman dropping off the mail, call out to him, "Hey, thank you. I appreciate that." When you go to the grocery store, encourage the cashier. Be friendly. Sow a seed with the bank teller, the woman who cuts your hair, the man at the gas station; make a positive deposit in each of their lives as you pass their way.

"Why bother?" you may ask. "I'm never going to have a long-term relationship with them."

Maybe not, but as part of your relationship with God, you can still extend kindness and appreciation to every person you meet. Scripture says, "We should encourage one another daily" (see Hebrews 3:13). That means every day you should find somebody you can help build up. Each day look for somebody for whom you can make a deposit of encouragement. A simple compliment may turn somebody's whole day around. "You look great today. That color really looks good on you." Or you can tell somebody, "I appreciate you being my friend. That means a lot to me."

I remember when I was at my father's house and he would see the mailman coming, Daddy would get a big smile on his face and say, "Well, look-ee here, here comes the finest mailman in all the world." That mailman's countenance would light up. My father's simple compliment brightened the man's day. It didn't take a lot of effort; it didn't require much of Daddy's time. He had developed a habit of investing in people, in helping other people to feel better about themselves.

> As part of your relationship with God, you can extend kindness and appreciation to every person you meet.

Your words have the power to put a spring in somebody's step, to lift somebody out of defeat and discouragement, and to help propel someone to victory. A potentially uplifting deposit such as Daddy made in the life of that postman doesn't take much more than ten or fifteen seconds to make. Yet those in your realm of influence may need just such a fifteen-second investment in the accounts they share with you.

Understand that every person needs encouragement, no matter who he or she is or how successful he or she appears to be. Frequently, someone will tell me, "Joel, you've really helped me," or, "You've made such a difference in my life." Every time I hear a statement such as that, it encourages me to be better; it does something deep down on the inside of me that lets me know that my life has significance and that I've been able to make a difference in this world. Everyone you know needs that sort of encouragement.

Husband, your wife can never hear you say too many times, "You're beautiful. I think you're great. I'm so glad that you're my wife." Keep those emotional accounts growing.

Learn to give compliments freely. Learn to be friendly, and avoid anything that exudes the attitude that you are so important that you can't take time for somebody who's not up to your level. Instead, make everyone you meet feel important; strive to make every person with whom you have contact feel special. After all, every person you meet is made in the image of God.

❧ Today's Prayer to Become a Better You ❧

Father, help me remember that investing compliments never diminishes my supply but increases it! Help me be more intentional about spreading encouragement to each person I meet—for Your sake.

❧ Today's Thought to Become a Better You ❧

Investing in my neighbor's life is a central part of what God designed me to do.

BLESS SOMEONE ELSE

*May God be merciful and bless us. May his face smile
with favor on us.*

Psalm 67:1

Do you want to get more out of life? Who doesn't, right? Okay,
try this: Get up every day and, rather than trying to be blessed, do
everything in your power to be a blessing to someone else. If you will
do that for six weeks—trying to be a blessing to someone every
day—your life will be filled with so many blessings you won't be able
to contain them all.

I've discovered that if I meet other people's needs, God will
meet mine. If I make somebody else happy, God will make sure
that I'm happy. Every day, we should look for opportunities to be
good to people. Maybe you can buy somebody's lunch, or give
someone a ride, babysit somebody's children, tip a little more
than is expected. Get in a habit of doing some good for somebody
every day. Don't make the mistake of living selfishly. That's one of
the worst prisons you could ever live in. You were not created to
be focused only on yourself. Almighty God made you to be a
giver. The best way for you to be fulfilled is to get your mind off
yourself and reach out to others.

Get up in the morning with this attitude: "Who can I be a blessing to today? Who can I encourage? Where is there a need that I can
meet?"

I don't believe we see enough good works today. We hear a lot about success and about the good things that God wants to do for us, but let's not forget we are blessed so we can be a blessing. We are blessed so we can share God's goodness wherever we go. If you want

> If I meet other people's needs, God will meet mine.

to make an impact on somebody's life, you don't necessarily have to preach a sermon to that person; just be good to him. Your actions will speak much louder than your words. You can say, "I love you and I care about you," but we demonstrate true love by what we do.

If I love you, I'll go out of my way to help you. If I love you, I'll give you a ride to work or school, even though I have to get up earlier than usual to do it. If I love you, I'll babysit your children when I know you're not feeling well. True love turns words and feelings into action.

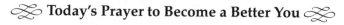 Today's Prayer to Become a Better You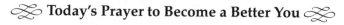

Father, I can't wait to meet the people You put in my way today just so I can have the joy of blessing them whether they realize it or not!

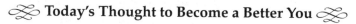 Today's Thought to Become a Better You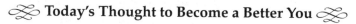

Who can I be a blessing to today?

TAKING TIME TO DO GOOD

SCRIPTURE READING TO BECOME A BETTER YOU   Mark 10:13–16

Let the children come to me. Don't stop them! For the Kingdom of God belongs to those who are like these children.

MARK 10:14

Scripture says that in the last days the love of the great body of people will grow cold (see 2 Timothy 3:1–5). That simply means that people will be so busy, they'll be so focused on their own needs, they'll be so caught up in their drive for success they won't take time to make a difference in someone else's life.

Friend, don't let that description apply to you. All around you people are hurting. They need your love and your encouragement. Don't miss the miracle of the moment. You may have someone in your life right now who needs your time and energy. Are you paying attention?

Maybe one of your coworkers is just about on the brink of giving up. He desperately needs your encouragement. She needs you to take her to lunch and let her know that you care. Don't be too busy. Don't be insensitive to the needs around you. Be willing to be inconvenienced.

When you study the life of Jesus, you'll notice that He always took time for people. He was busy. He had places He wanted to go, but He was always willing to change His plans to do good for somebody else. As He walked through the villages, people called out to Him, "Jesus, please come over here and pray for us." He would stop and go out of His way to bring healing to those people. One time they came up to Him and said, "Jesus, please come to our city, our relative is so sick. You've got to pray for him." Jesus changed His plans and went that way.

Don't miss the miracle of the moment.

When they tried to bring the little children to Jesus, the disciples said, "No, don't bother Him. He's busy. He's too important."

Jesus said, "No, no; let the children come to Me."

It's so easy for us to get caught up in our own little worlds and focus only on ourselves. "I've got my plans. Don't get me off my schedule." Instead, take time for people. Don't miss any opportunities to do good. Make a difference in somebody's life. It doesn't have to be something big. Often, small gestures of love and kindness can make a big difference. A women's group at our church makes blankets, and then the women embroider Scripture verses on them and take them to cancer patients at M. D. Anderson Cancer Center, in Houston. Those handmade blankets remind the men and women struggling with cancer that somebody cares; the expression of love gives them an extra ray of hope. Those ladies are using their talents to do something good for somebody else.

You may not have a lot of extra money, but maybe you can make a blanket or bake a cake. You can mentor a young man. You can visit the nursing home. You can get involved in a prison outreach and encourage the inmates to trust God. Do something good for somebody.

O. A. "Bum" Phillips, the legendary NFL football coach, retired from the game a number of years ago, but Phillips isn't really retired. He's at the prisons every chance he gets, encouraging the prisoners and giving them hope. That's what life's all about—doing something good for somebody else. John Bunyan, the author of the classic

Pilgrim's Progress, said, "You have not lived today until you have done something for someone who can never repay you."

✺ Today's Prayer to Become a Better You ✺

Father, thank You for Jesus' example of someone who took time for others. I want His pattern to be the pattern in my life.

✺ Today's Thought to Become a Better You ✺

I am imitating God most closely when I give.

PART FOUR

FORM BETTER HABITS

FEED GOOD HABITS

SCRIPTURE READING TO BECOME A BETTER YOU
1 Corinthians 10:23–11:1

*Don't be concerned for your own good but for the good
of others.*

1 CORINTHIANS 10:24

To BECOME A BETTER YOU, take inventory of your habits. Do you
have a tendency to be negative in your thoughts and conversations?
Are you always late to work? Do you worry all the time? Do you
overeat? Do you regularly succumb to addictions?

Understand, your habit may not be legally, ethically, or morally
wrong. It can be a seemingly innocuous action or attitude, a little
thing, but if you don't do something about it, you can go for years
wasting time and energy, being unproductive and unprofitable. That
is not God's best.

The good news is, you can change. You can develop better habits.
Most studies of habitual behavior indicate that a habit can be broken in six weeks; some studies tell us that you can break a habit in
as little as twenty-one days. Think about that. If you will discipline
yourself for a month or so and be willing to suffer through the
pain of change, you can rid yourself of a negative behavior, form a
new healthy habit, and rise to a new level of personal freedom.

The apostle Paul said, "All things are permissible to me, but not
all things are profitable. All things are lawful, but I will not be
mastered by anything." Notice, Paul is saying in effect, "I'm going to

rid myself of anything that is not profitable or productive in my life." He was saying, "I'm not going to stay under the control of any bad habits."

It's a fact: Successful people develop better habits. That's why even

People who get ahead in life usually get there on time.

professional golfers practice hitting golf balls nearly every day. Some pros hit as many as five hundred to a thousand balls a day when they are not competing in tournaments. They work for hours to repeat their golf swing so they can do it without even thinking about it. Then, when they get in a tournament under intense pressure, their bodies perform the correct swing almost automatically. No wonder those golfers are successful! They have formed successful habits.

If you have a bad habit of not getting to work on time, change that behavior. People who get ahead in life are usually punctual. Get up fifteen minutes earlier on days you must go to work, attend school, or go to a meeting. Plan your travel so you can arrive with time to spare. Establish a new routine of being on time. Don't allow yourself to be late when punctuality is such an easy habit to develop. Or if you have a habit of eating a bunch of junk food and drinking several sodas every day, commit yourself to forming better eating habits. Don't go on a crash diet; just change one small thing at a time. Before long, you will notice a marked difference in your energy level as well as your personal appearance.

❧ Today's Prayer to Become a Better You ❧

Father, guide me as I examine my daily routine for bad habits. With Your help I intend to replace at least one of them with a positive, uplifting habit.

≈ Today's Thought to Become a Better You ≈

I can encourage my own good habits!

HABITS AND CHARACTER

Scripture Reading to Become a Better You   Galatians 5:16–25

Since we are living by the Spirit, let us follow the Spirit's leading in every part of our lives.

Galatians 5:25

Our habits become part of our character. If you allow yourself to be disorganized or you are always running late, that becomes a part of who you are. If you've trained yourself to get upset and have a fit whenever you don't get your way, unfortunately those bad habits become a part of you too. The first step toward changing is to identify what's holding you back. Identify any bad habits, and then make a decision to do something about them.

How do we change a habit? Simple: Quit feeding the bad habit. You have to starve your bad habits into submission and start nourishing your good habits.

I heard somebody say, "Bad habits are easy to develop but difficult to live with." In other words, it's easy to pop off and be rude, saying whatever you feel and making snide, cutting, sarcastic remarks. That's easy. But it's difficult to live in a home filled with strife and tension.

It's easy to spend money that we don't have and charge everything on our credit cards. It's hard to live with the pressure of not being able to pay our bills. It's easy to give in to temptation and do whatever we feel like doing. It's difficult to live in bondage, feeling guilty and condemned.

Consider a person with a chemical addiction. It is easy to get hooked. It may seem fun and exciting at first. Before long, however, that addiction controls the person. He becomes a slave to it. Bad habits are easy to acquire but hard to live with.

On the other hand, good habits are difficult to develop. A good habit results from a desire to work and sacrifice and, sometimes, a willingness to endure pain and suffering. But good habits are easy to live with. For instance, at first it's

**Good habits
are easy to live with.**

hard to hold your tongue and overlook an offense when someone criticizes or insults you. It's hard at first to forgive. But it sure is easy to live in a home filled with peace and harmony.

If you are willing to be uncomfortable for a little while, so you can press past the initial pain of change, in the long run your life will be much better. Pain doesn't last forever; in fact, once you develop the new habit, the pain often disappears.

Victoria knows that I won't argue with her. We don't allow strife and conflict in our home. In our marriage, it's not hard for me to overlook things or to forgive an offense, because I've simply trained myself to be a peacemaker. I've trained myself to apologize even when it's not my fault, which of course is every time we have a disagreement!

However, in the early years of our marriage, I didn't respond that way. Instead, I'd put up a good argument, and I'd tell her what I thought and the way I felt it should be. One day I realized, *That's not the way God wants me to live.* That's not His best. I could hear the still, small voice down inside, saying, *Joel, let it go. You're better than this. Don't live on this low level.*

I recognized that I had to make a decision: Did I want to prove I was right, or did I want to have peace in our home? I began to change, and relinquishing my right to fight gradually got easier. Today, it's not difficult at all for me to be easygoing; it has become part of my character. It's natural to me. Truth is, I could still be floundering where I was twenty years ago, when Victoria and I first married: arguing, pouting when I didn't get my way, and always wanting to have the last word.

Thankfully, I developed better habits. I pressed past the pain of change, and today I can say it has been worth it. Sure, I have other areas in which I need to improve—maybe one or two!

If you, too, will press past the initial pain—whether it takes a week, a month, or a year—eventually the pain will go away, and you will not only enjoy your life a lot more, but you'll be living at a much higher level.

∻ Today's Prayer to Become a Better You ∻

Father, I'm ready to enjoy some good habits. Thank You for giving me the choice to live at a higher level. What a great gift!

∻ Today's Thought to Become a Better You ∻

I will press past the pain of change to develop some good habits.

TIME FOR A CHANGE

SCRIPTURE READING TO BECOME A BETTER YOU

1 Corinthians 10:12–13

The temptations in your life are no different from what others experience. And God is faithful. He will not allow the temptation to be more than you can stand. When you are tempted, he will show you a way out so that you can endure.

1 CORINTHIANS 10:13

JUST AS SOME PEOPLE don't manage their diets well, others don't manage their time well. They're not living balanced lives; consequently they are stressed out, always run-down. They've gotten into a habit of overworking. They rarely relax; they hardly ever exercise. They never take any free time for themselves. Unless they make changes and bring some balance into their lives, one day that's going to catch up to them. You can live stressed out for a while, especially when you're young. But don't be surprised when your body suffers the consequences.

It's much better to develop good habits right now. Look at the way you live, and ask, "Why am I doing what I'm doing? Is this something that's been passed down to me by my family? Is this a good habit? Is it helping me become a better person?" If, in your analysis, you discover some habits that are not productive or profitable, dare to make the changes that will help you to replace them. Make sure you're not allowing anything but God to master you.

You will always have plenty of excuses and rationalizations why you should not change. You can usually find a reason to give up, turn around, go back, and keep living the same way you've always lived. Don't be surprised when you are tested. Simply remember that Scripture says, "There is no temptation that will come to you that you can't overcome. God will always make a way of escape" (see 1 Corinthians 10:13). No matter how intense the pressure or how difficult it seems, you need to know that you can withstand it. God will help you. He will make a way of escape, but you must take it.

It's not so much that we break bad habits; we must replace them.

If you see an area where you're not responding in a positive manner, don't make excuses. Take responsibility and say, "I recognize what's happening, and I choose to change. I'm going to develop better habits."

In reality, it's not so much that we *break* bad habits; we must *replace* them. In other words, if you have a problem with worry, and your mind is always racing ninety miles per hour—worried about your children, worried about your finances, worried about your health—you need to recognize that worry is a bad habit you've developed. It is hard to worry and trust God at the same time. God wants your mind to be at peace. You can rest assured, knowing that God has you in the palm of His hand. When you've been worrying for a long time, however, it's almost second nature to you; you don't even think about it. You just get up in the morning and start worrying about what the day will bring.

In most cases, you can't simply decide to stop worrying. You have to replace the negative thoughts with positive faith-filled thoughts. Then every time you're tempted to worry, use that temptation as a reminder to dwell on good things. Scripture tells us to "Dwell on things that are pure, things that are wholesome, things that are of a good report" (see Philippians 4:8). If you will replace those thoughts of worry with thoughts of hope, faith, and victory, then you will retrain your mind. Do that day in and day out, and before long, you will have formed a habit of dwelling on good things, and you'll have broken that old habit of worry.

❧ Today's Prayer to Become a Better You ❧

Father, thank You for the encouragement that habits can be replaced. You have given me hope. I realize I need to focus on the good habits You want me to develop rather than being distracted by old bad habits. I want to live for You.

❧ Today's Thought to Become a Better You ❧

When I replace a bad habit, I can remember it without having to repeat it.

FREEDOM FROM BAD HABITS

Keep watch and pray, so that you will not give in to temptation. For the spirit is willing, but the body is weak!
MATTHEW 26:41

THE FIRST STEP to overcoming any habit or addiction is to identify what's holding you back. But don't stop there. Make a decision to do something about it. Take action. Don't be too embarrassed to seek help. People struggle with chemical addictions, sexual addictions, and all sorts of other maladies. It may be an anger addiction. You just can't control your temper. Understand that you can change. Freedom is available. Don't believe the lie that you're stuck and you'll never get any better. God already has a path of success laid out for you.

But you must do your part and be willing to walk it out. The next time that temptation comes, the first thing you should do is pray. Get God involved in your situation. We cannot defeat bad habits in our own strength. Ask God to help you. When you feel your emotions getting out of hand, and you are tempted to rudely tell somebody off, pray right then and there, under your breath, *God, I'm asking You to help me. Give me the grace to keep my mouth closed and the courage to walk away.*

Scripture tells us, "Pray that you don't come into temptation" (see Matthew 26:41). It doesn't say, "Pray that you'll never be tempted."

We're all going to face temptation. God says, "When that temptation comes, ask Me for my help." In any area that you're trying to change—even small things—seek His help. "God, I'm about to walk through this kitchen, and I can smell the chocolate-chip cookies, so I'm asking You to help me resist the temptation to break my diet." "Father, all my friends are going out partying tonight, and I know down inside, it's not right. God, I'm asking You to help me make the best choice. Help me stay on Your best plan."

Get God involved in your situation.

"Joel, that's difficult. It's hard not to go out with my friends, hard not to use my credit cards, hard not to speak my mind."

Yes, that's difficult. But living in bondage is even more difficult. Feeling bad about yourself because you know you're living below your potential is even harder. There's nothing worse than going through the day with little things holding you back that you know good and well you can beat.

Maybe you are struggling with addictions, or you battle with your temper or impatience. Possibly, you are living in mediocrity, simply because you are allowing something small to control you. Let me tell you what you already know: You are better than that. You are a child of the Most High God. You have His royal blood flowing through your veins. Don't just sit back and settle where you are. No obstacle in your life—large or small—is insurmountable. It doesn't matter whether it's a critical spirit or an addiction to cocaine. God's power in you is greater than the power that's trying to hold you back. Fight the good fight of faith. Don't let anything or anyone on earth master you. Your attitude should be, "That's it. I'm not staying where I am. I'm moving up higher. I know I'm better than this."

Tap into God's power within you and stop saying, "I can't break that habit." Instead, start declaring every day: "I am free. I can do all things through Christ. No weapon formed against me is ever going to prosper." Remember what Jesus said: "Whom the Son sets free is free indeed." Start declaring that over your own life.

⋙ Today's Prayer to Become a Better You ⋘

Father, I am truly free because of Christ. Because of Him, no weapon formed against me is ever going to prosper. In Christ's strength I can leave bad habits behind.

⋙ Today's Thought to Become a Better You ⋘

I will fight the good fight of faith.

HABITUAL HAPPINESS

SCRIPTURE READING TO BECOME A BETTER YOU

1 Thessalonians 5:12–22

Always be joyful.

1 THESSALONIANS 5:16

MANY PEOPLE DON'T REALIZE that much of the manner in which we approach life—our attitudes and our demeanor—is learned behavior. These habits have formed by repetition throughout the years. If we've spent years focusing on what's wrong rather than what's right, then these negative patterns are going to keep us from enjoying our lives.

We acquired many of our habits from our parents or from the people who were around us as we grew up. Studies tell us that negative parents raise negative children. If your parents focused more on what was wrong, living stressed out, uptight, or discouraged, there's a good possibility that you have developed some of those same negative mind-sets.

I often have people tell me, "Well, Joel, I'm just a worrier. I'm just uptight. I'm not a friendly sort of person."

No, please understand, those are habits that you have developed. And the good news is you can "reprogram" your own "computer." You can get rid of a negative mentality and develop a habit of happiness.

The Bible says, "Rejoice in the Lord always" (see 1 Thessalonians 5:16). One translation simply says, "Be happy all the time." That means no matter what comes our way, we can have smiles on our faces. We should get up each morning excited about that day. Even if we are facing difficult or negative circumstances, we need to learn to keep a positive outlook.

> Happiness does not depend on your circumstances. . . . It's a choice that you make.

Many people are waiting for their circumstances to be worked out before they decide to be happy. "Joel, as soon as I get a better job . . . ; as soon as my child straightens up . . . ; as soon as my health improves . . ."

No, the bottom line is, if you're going to be happy, you need to make a decision to be happy right now.

Happiness does not depend on your circumstances; it depends on your will. It's a choice that you make. I've seen people go through some of the most awful, unfortunate situations, yet at the time you would never know they were having problems. They had smiles on their faces and good reports on their lips. In spite of their dire dilemmas, they remained positive, upbeat, and energetic.

Other people in similar circumstances—and some in far less severe situations—insist on wallowing in despair; they're down, depressed, discouraged, and worried. What makes the difference?

It's all in how they've trained their minds. One person has developed a habit of happiness. She is hopeful, trusting, believing for the best. The other person has trained his mind to see the negative. He's worried, frustrated, and constantly complaining.

If you are going to develop a habit of happiness, you must learn to relax and go with the flow, instead of getting frustrated. You have to believe that God is in control, and that means you have no need to be stressed out and worried. Moreover, you have to be grateful for what you have, rather than complaining about what you don't have. A habit of happiness boils down to staying on the positive side of life.

Each day is full of surprises and inconveniences, so you must accept the fact that not everything is going to always go your way. Your plans are not always going to work out just as you scheduled them. When that happens, make a willful decision that you are not going to let the circumstances upset you. Don't allow stress to steal your joy. Instead, be adaptable and adjustable and seek to make the best of a bad situation.

One of the best things I've ever learned is that I don't have to have my way to be happy. I've made up my mind that I'm going to enjoy each day whether my plans work out, or whether they don't.

Our attitude should be, "I'm going to enjoy today even if I have a flat tire on the way home. I'm going to enjoy each day even if it rains out my ball game. I'm going to be happy in life even if I don't get that promotion that I was hoping for."

When you have that kind of attitude, minor irritations or inconveniences that may have stressed you out will cease to be a source of frustration. You don't have to live all uptight. Understand, you can't control people, nor can you change them. Only God can do that. If somebody is doing something that's getting on your nerves, you might as well leave that up to God. Quit allowing somebody else's quirk or idiosyncrasy to get the best of you.

❧ Today's Prayer to Become a Better You ❧

Father, I realize that choosing to be joyful is a clear way I can express my faith in You. Since You are in control of the events in my life and have my good in mind, I'm making the choice to practice happiness today.

❧ Today's Thought to Become a Better You ❧

Ten years from now, I won't even remember many of the things that are causing me stress today.

DIRECTED ATTENTION

Scripture Reading to Become a Better You   Philippians 3:12–14

I focus on this one thing: Forgetting the past and looking forward to what lies ahead, I press on to reach the end of the race and receive the heavenly prize for which God, through Christ Jesus, is calling us.

PHILIPPIANS 3:13–14

UNQUESTIONABLY, what you put into your heart and mind is what you're going to get out of it. Sure, you may have negative circumstances. Maybe you didn't get good breaks. Maybe you didn't get the position you were longing for. Now instead of automatically stamping it "negative" and storing it away, turn your attitude around. Remind yourself, *I know God has something better in store for me. I know when one door closes, God can open another door.* When you do that, you will take that negative situation, turn it around, and stamp it "positive."

You can do this even in your most difficult times. Maybe you lost a loved one. I know that can be painful, but our attitude should be, "I know where she is. She's in a better place, a place of joy, a place of peace." When we do that, we're stamping that experience as a "positive."

Pay attention to what you're feeding yourself. Are you storing away more positives or more negatives? You cannot mentally brand everything as negative and expect to live a positive, happy life. For example:

"I got caught in traffic last week, and I missed an important meeting."

No, turn it around and declare, "Father, I thank you that you have me at the right place at the right time. I am not going to get depressed. I believe you're directing my steps and you're going to turn that missed meeting around and use it for my good."

When you do that, you're turning around a negative and stamping it positive. In the process, as you grow more accustomed to this sort of mind-set, you will discover that you are developing a habit of happiness.

You cannot mentally brand everything as negative and expect to live a positive, happy life.

Our brain possesses a fascinating function known as the "reticular activating system." It's a function through which our minds eliminate the thoughts and the impulses deemed unnecessary. For instance, years ago my sister Lisa lived in a townhome right beside the railroad tracks. Two or three times a night, a train rumbled by, loudly sounding its whistle as it passed her window. That train literally shook the place. When Lisa first moved in, the train awakened her no matter how deeply she was sleeping. But after living there for several weeks, an amazing thing happened. Those trains could pass by in the middle of the night, and Lisa would hardly even notice. Several months later, Lisa was able to sleep all through the night.

One time, I stayed at her house, and that train came by in the middle of the night. I think I jumped three feet off the bed. It sounded like the world was coming to an end.

The next morning, I asked Lisa, "How do you sleep here with that train going by in the night?"

"What train?" she asked.

The reticular activating system in her mind processed the sound of the train going by and allowed her to sleep right through it.

In a similar manner, we can train our minds in such a positive fashion that when negative, discouraging thoughts come, they won't affect us anymore. When that thought of fear comes, learn to tune it out as Lisa did. Or that depressing thought, *It's going to be a lousy day*—tune it out. If you'll keep it up, before long, your mind's reticular activating system says, *He doesn't need this information. She's not paying attention. Don't even send the thought of fear or worry.*

Certainly, that is an oversimplification of the mental process, but just as Lisa was able to tune out the sounds of that train, I believe we can tune out negative messages. We can tune in to thoughts of joy, peace, faith, hope, and victory as we learn to turn around negatives and stamp everything positive.

"Well, Joel, my children are not doing well. They've gotten off course. I'm so worried about them." No, just turn that around: "Father, thank you that my children are blessed, they're making good decisions. I declare what Your Word says, 'As for me and my house, we will serve the LORD.' "

"Well, Joel, it's my finances. Gas prices are so high. Business is slow. I don't see how I'm going to make it."

No, tune that out and start tuning in, "God is supplying all of my needs. Everything I touch prospers and succeeds. I am blessed. I cannot be cursed."

Train your mind to see the good. Get rid of any negative, conditioned responses. Everybody around you may be complaining, but you can find the good in every situation. If you'll do what Scripture says, you can indeed be happy at all times.

❧ Today's Prayer to Become a Better You ❧

Thank You, Father, for the gift of the reticular activating system! It reminds me that You always make it possible to live the way You want me to live.

❧ Today's Thought to Become a Better You ❧

I am able to change any negative label to a positive one.

HANDLING CRITICISM

SCRIPTURE READING TO BECOME A BETTER YOU   Genesis 50:14–21

You intended to harm me, but God intended it all for good. He brought me to this position so I could save the lives of many people.

GENESIS 50:20

EVERY ONE OF US will have times when we are criticized, sometimes fairly, but more often unfairly, creating stress in our hearts and minds and tension in our relationships. Somebody at work or in your social circle speaks negatively about you or blames you for something, trying to make you look bad or blowing some minor incident out of proportion. Usually, your critics have no interest in helping you; they are simply trying to drag you down.

Certainly, constructive criticism can be helpful. An insightful point of light presented by someone who truly has your best interests at heart can illuminate an area where you need to improve. Sad to say, most criticism is not intended to build up another person; quite the opposite. It is not given in the spirit of blessing, but is more often presented with an intentional sting. The criticism that hurts the worst is frequently undeserved and unfair. Such criticism is a reflection more of the critic than of the person being criticized.

I've found that unwarranted criticism is most often based on jealousy. It stems from a competitive spirit. You have something that somebody else wants. Instead of being happy for you, instead of keeping a good attitude, knowing that God can do something similar for anyone who trusts Him, jealousy rises up in the critical person. Critics try to cover their own insecurity by being critical, cynical, caustic, or snippy toward others.

The more successful you are, the more criticism you will encounter. If you get that promotion at the office, don't be surprised when your critics come out of the woodwork.

The key to handling criticism: Never take it personally.

"Well, he's not that talented," someone might say. "She's just a manipulator, always playing up to the boss."

Or your friends may be fine as long as you are single. Once you are married, however, they start saying things such as, "I can't believe he married her. She has no personality whatsoever."

Unfortunately, not everybody will celebrate your victories with you. Not all your single friends may jump up and down when you marry the man of your dreams. Your coworkers may not sing your praises when you get that promotion. Sadly, for some people your success evokes that jealous, critical spirit rather than appreciation and compliments.

Here's the key to handling criticism: Never take it personally. Many times, it's not even about you, even though it may be directed at you. If the critic weren't tearing you apart, he'd be complaining about somebody else. It's something on the inside of the critical person that lashes out at others. Unless she deals with it, it's going to keep her from rising higher.

One of the most important things I've ever learned is to celebrate other people's victories. If your coworker gets the promotion you wanted, yes, there is a tendency to be jealous. Sure, there's a tendency to think, *Why didn't that happen for me? I work hard. That's not fair.*

However, if we'll keep the right attitude and be happy for other people's success, at the right time God will open up something even better for us. I've found that if I can't rejoice with others, I'm not going to get to where I want to be. Many times, God has a promotion in store, but first He sends along a test. He wants to see if we're ready. When our best friends get married, while we're still single, can we be happy for them? Or when our relatives move into their dream house, and we've been praying for years to own a home but are still renting a crowded apartment, will we be glad for them? That's a test. If you get jealous and critical, your attitude will trap you right where you are. Learn to celebrate

**Celebrate
other people's victories.**

other people's victories. Let their successes inspire you. Know that if God did something so marvelous for them, He can certainly do it for you.

∽ Today's Prayer to Become a Better You ∽

Please bless my critics today, Father. Help me to recognize any truth they have to share, and to reject anything that is unlike You.

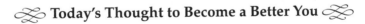

∽ Today's Thought to Become a Better You ∽

I choose never to take a criticism personally.

HANDLING THE SLINGERS

Scripture Reading to Become a Better You   Matthew 10:5–15

If any household or town refuses to welcome you or listen to your message, shake its dust from your feet as you leave.

MATTHEW 10:14

IF YOU ARE GOING to become better, you will need to know how to deal with critics—people who are talking about you, judging you, or maybe even making false accusations. In Old Testament times, these people were called "slingers." When an enemy attacked a city, their first priority was to pry the stones off the wall protecting that city. They would then sling those stones into the city's wells. The attackers knew if they could clog the wells with stones and interrupt the flow of water, eventually the people within the walls would have to come out.

Do you see the parallel? You have a well of good things on the inside, a well of joy, peace, and victory. Too often, we let the slingers clog up our wells. Perhaps somebody speaks derogatorily about you, but instead of letting it go, you dwell on it, growing more and more upset. Before long, you think, *I'm going to get even; I'm going to pay them back. They are speaking untruths about me; let me tell you what I know about them.*

Instead, make it a priority to keep your well pure. If somebody is critical of you, trying to show you in a bad light, recognize that as a stone coming your way. If you dwell on it or get upset and revengeful, the person who threw that stone has accomplished his or her goal. Another stone landed in your well. Now your joy, peace, and victory become more restricted. They don't flow like they should.

Truth is, we all have some slingers in our lives, people who try to bring us down with their words or actions. They may be friends to your face, but you know behind your back they would shred you if given an opportunity.

The way you overcome unwarranted criticism is by not allowing yourself to take revenge or even harboring an attitude that wants revenge. Don't sink down to your critics' level and start

Sometimes when you leave the workplace at the end of the day, you simply have to shake it off.

talking badly about them. Most of all, don't get defensive or try to prove that you're right and they're wrong. No, the way you defeat a slinger is to shake him or her off and keep moving forward. Keep your eyes on the prize; stay focused on your goals, and do what you believe God wants you to do.

This is what Jesus told His disciples to do when He sent them out to various towns to teach the people, to heal the sick, and to care for their needs. Jesus knew His followers would sometimes suffer rejection. Not everybody would like them or gladly receive their message. Some people would get jealous and start talking negatively about them, trying to make them look bad. Jesus knew the slingers would be out there, so He instructed His disciples, "When you go into a town, whoever will not receive and welcome your message, when you leave that place, shake the dust off of your feet" (see Matthew 10:14).

Jesus did not advise *if* they treat you poorly, *if* they start talking about you and spreading rumors; He said *when* they do these things. Jesus did not advise His disciples to become defensive or worried. Neither did He instruct them to defend their reputations and set the record straight. He simply said, "Shake the dust off of your feet."

That was a symbolic way of saying, "You're not going to steal my joy. You may reject me or speak badly about me, but I'm not going to sink down to your level. I'm not going to fight with you. I'm going to let God be my vindicator."

Sometimes when you leave the workplace at the end of the day, you simply have to shake it off. People's backbiting, playing politics, trying to bring you down—leave it; don't lug that heavy, worthless load home. Shake it off. Sometimes even when leaving a relative's house, you may have to say, "I'm shaking this off. I'm not going to drink of their poison."

Let God be your vindicator. If you'll stay on the high road, God will fight your battles for you. You never really win by sinking down to your critics' level and attacking them personally. Rise above that.

When somebody is critical or negative toward you, your attitude should be, "I'm better than that. I'm not going to let this person's stone clog up my well. I'm not going to let that jealous spirit poison my life. I'm going to stay full of joy."

⬥ Today's Prayer to Become a Better You ⬥

Father, thank You for the reminder that I can "shake it off." I don't have to carry negativity or criticism with me but can leave it behind in Your capable hands.

⬥ Today's Thought to Become a Better You ⬥

Part of the victory is "shaking it off."

RUN YOUR OWN RACE

Scripture Reading to Become a Better You   Matthew 9:9–13

[Jesus] added, "Now go and learn the meaning of this Scripture: 'I want you to show mercy, not offer sacrifices.' For I have come to call not those who think they are righteous, but those who know they are sinners."

MATTHEW 9:13

RECOGNIZE THAT YOU cannot stop people from talking negatively. If you are trying to be the "gossip police," hoping to make sure that nobody ever says a negative thing about you, you're going to live a frustrated life. No, accept the fact that certain people are going to make cutting remarks. But you are better than that; you don't have to drink of their poison. You can rise above it. You can stay on the high road and enjoy your life anyway.

I don't have time to sit around thinking about all the people who don't like me. I realize that every day is a gift from God, and my time is too valuable to waste it trying to please everybody. No, I've accepted the fact that not everybody is going to like me and not everybody is going to understand me. You don't have to try to explain yourself. Don't spend time trying to win over your critics; just run your own race.

I start every morning searching my own heart. I make sure, to the best of my ability, that I'm doing what I believe God wants me to do. As I follow Scripture and feel in my own heart that my life is on course, that's all that matters. I can't afford to let critics and negative voices distract me—and neither can you!

Some people spend more time focused on what other people are saying about them than they do thinking about their own dreams and goals. But understand that if you're going to do anything great in life—whether you want to be a great teacher, a successful businessperson, or a champion athlete—not everybody is going to be your cheerleader. Not everybody is going to be excited about your dream. In fact, some people are going to be downright jealous. They will find fault and criticize. It is crucial that you learn to shake off unwarranted criticism, because the moment you start changing so you can please people, you will be taking a step backward. Sure, you could say, "I'm not going to show up early at work anymore, because my coworkers are starting to talk about me," or, "I'm not going to buy that car that I really want, because I know people are going to judge; people are going to condemn me." No, I've found that no matter what you do or don't do, somebody won't like it, so don't waste your time worrying about it. Do what God has put in your heart, and trust Him to take care of the critics.

Don't spend time trying to win over your critics; just run your own race.

Maybe you need to get free from trying to please everybody. Stop worrying that somebody might criticize you. Remember that if you are criticized when you are trying to make a positive difference in the world, you're in good company. Jesus was perpetually criticized for doing good. He was even criticized for healing a man on the Sabbath. He was criticized for going to dinner with a tax collector. The critics called Him a friend of sinners. He was criticized for helping a woman in need, somebody they were about to stone. Jesus didn't change His ways in a futile attempt to fit into everybody's mold. He didn't try to explain Himself and make everybody understand Him; He stayed focused and fulfilled His destiny.

This truth really helped to set me free. There was a time in my life when I wanted everybody to like me. If I heard one negative comment, I thought, *Oh, no. I've failed. What have I done wrong? What do I need to change?*

One day I realized it's impossible for everybody to like me, and if someone chooses to misinterpret my message or my motives, there's nothing I can do about it anyhow. Now I don't let my critics upset me or steal my joy. I know most of the time it's not about me. The success God has given me stirs up the jealousy in them.

*Jesus . . .
stayed focused
and fulfilled
His destiny.*

If you're making a difference in your family or at the office or in your workplace, you will always have your share of critics. Don't allow them to stress you out. Simply recognize that the higher you go, the more visible a target you will be and the more critics will want to take shots at you.

✣ Today's Prayer to Become a Better You ✣

Father, help me realize when I'm wasting time trying to please others instead of pleasing You by becoming a better me! I know You will always help me run my own race.

✣ Today's Thought to Become a Better You ✣

I have a particular race laid out for me to run today. I'm going to stay on the track.

GOD HAS THE FINAL SAY

Scripture Reading to Become a Better You   Acts 18:1–11

When they opposed and insulted him, Paul shook the dust from his clothes and said, "Your blood is upon your own heads—I am innocent. From now on I will go preach to the Gentiles."

ACTS 18:6

DURING HIS EXTENSIVE TRAVELS throughout the Roman world, the apostle Paul often had great crowds following him. And time and time again, people became jealous; they got all stirred up and on several occasions ran him out of town. What did Paul do? Did he get depressed and say, "God, I'm trying to do my best, but nobody understands me"? No, he shook the dust off his feet. He was saying in effect, "It's your loss, not mine, because I'm going to do great things for God. I'm not going to allow your rejection or your negative words to keep me from my destiny." His attitude was, "Sling all you want to. I have a cover on my well. I'm not going to let you poison my life." I heard somebody say, "If people run you out of town, just get to the front of the line and act like you're leading the parade." In other words, shake it off and keep moving forward.

I love the scripture that says "No weapon formed against us will prosper, but every tongue raised against us in judgment, You will show to be in the wrong" (see Isaiah 54:17). You may have to endure some people's speaking against you, but if you can just stay on the high road and keep doing your best, you will prove their criticism invalid. Moreover, God will pour out His favor on you, in spite of your critics.

Understand that your destiny is not tied to what people are saying about you. Some critical people in Houston predicted that Lakewood Church would never be able to meet in the arena known as the Compaq Center. They told us we didn't have a chance. In fact, at a business luncheon attended by numerous high-level city leaders, one man told the people at his table, "It will be a cold day in hell before Lakewood Church ever gets the Compaq Center."

> Your destiny
> is not determined
> by your critics.

When I heard about that remark, I just shook it off. I knew our destiny was not tied to one dissenter. I knew that remark was nothing more than a distraction. I also realized that not everybody was going to understand our decision to move the church. I heard people saying, "Why do they need to move? Why do they want a bigger church? Why are they leaving their roots?" Many times, I was tempted to get in there and try to explain it, hoping to convince them that our moving was a good idea. I knew not everybody wanted to understand. And I guess there was a cold day in hell because Lakewood Church has now been worshiping God in the location formerly known as the Compaq Center since July 2005.

Friend, your destiny is not determined by your critics. God has the final say. Quit listening to what the naysayers are telling you, and stop living to please people. Shake that off and keep pressing forward in life.

❧ Today's Prayer to Become a Better You ❧

Father, You are the giver of dreams and direction. As long as I'm listening to You and following You, I don't have to worry about critics. Thanks for assuring me You have the final word.

⫘ **Today's Thought to Become a Better You** ⫘

Whatever happens today, God has the final say.

KEEP YOURSELF HAPPY

SCRIPTURE READING TO BECOME A BETTER YOU
2 Thessalonians 3:6–13

We hear that some of you are living idle lives, refusing to work and meddling in other people's business. We command such people and urge them in the name of the Lord Jesus Christ to settle down and work to earn their own living.

2 THESSALONIANS 3:11–12

ONE OF THE MOST important keys to a better life is to keep yourself happy, rather than living to please everybody else. It's easy to take on a false sense of responsibility, thinking that it is your job to keep everybody happy, to "fix" this person, to rescue that person, or to solve another person's problem.

Certainly, it is noble and admirable to want to help as many people as possible, and it is always good to reach out to others in need. Too often, though, we get out of balance. We're doing everything for everybody else, but we're not taking any time to keep ourselves healthy.

I've discovered that when I try to keep everybody around me happy by trying to meet all their needs, I'm the one who ends up suffering.

God does not want you to sacrifice your happiness to keep somebody else happy. At first brush, that may sound a little selfish, but there's a tenuous balance here. Your first priority is to take care of yourself. To do so, you must recognize that some people are still not going to be happy no matter what you do for them, no matter how nice you are, no matter how much time and energy you give them.

They have their own issues to deal with or things inside that they need to resolve.

All of us are responsible to keep ourselves happy.

Certainly there's a very fine line here, but you are not responsible for your spouse's happiness. Neither are you responsible for your children's happiness. All of us are responsible to keep ourselves happy.

If you are on the flip side of this issue, and you are the person who is doing the controlling, pardon me for being so blunt, but it is time for you to grow up and take responsibility for your own life. Quit relying on that other person to carry you. Quit demanding that your spouse cheer you up every day and work constantly to keep you encouraged. That's not fair to the other person. Stop manipulating that person when he or she does not comply with your wishes or do what you want. No, take responsibility and learn to keep yourself happy.

God has not called you to be unhappy simply to keep somebody else happy.

I'm not talking today about being selfish or self-centered. We should be givers. But there's a big difference between giving and allowing somebody to control you and make you feel guilty until you do what he or she wants. God has not called you to be unhappy simply to keep somebody else happy.

Again, if you are allowing that, the other person is not the only one at fault. You may have taken on a false sense of responsibility and now are allowing another person to control you.

If you are in a relationship where you do the majority of the giving and always encourage or rescue the other person, that is a clear sign that something is out of balance. You've become a crutch. And unless you make some changes, the relationship will continue to flounder.

You must take a stand. You can do it in love, but you need to go to that person and say, "I love you, but I'm not going to allow you to keep dumping your problems on me and making my life miserable. I'm not going to let you keep draining all my time and energy. You have to take responsibility and learn to keep yourself happy."

✆ Today's Prayer to Become a Better You ✆

Thank You, Father for challenging me to be responsible for my own happiness. Help me to preserve boundaries between myself and others that are healthy and helpful.

✆ Today's Thought to Become a Better You ✆

I'm not going to expect others to make me happy.

TURNING POINT

My brothers were angry with me; they forced me to care for their vineyards, so I couldn't care for myself—my own vineyard.

Song of Songs 1:6

It is liberating to understand that you don't have to keep everybody happy. More important, I really believe that if you live your life just trying to please people, you will not be able to fulfill your God-given destiny.

Sometimes you're not going to be able to keep everybody happy, even your closest loved ones. Of course, we should honor our parents, respect them, and listen to their advice. An intriguing Scripture verse, in the King James Version, says, "They have made me the keeper of the vineyards; but mine own vineyard have I not kept" (Song of Solomon 1:6). Solomon's bride was saying, "I was real good at keeping everybody else happy. I kept my parents happy; I kept my family happy; I took care of all my relatives and my friends. But in doing so, I neglected to take care of myself."

Too often, we live to please everybody else, but we neglect to take time to please ourselves. We end up allowing somebody else to run and control our lives.

If you allow them, some people will draw all your time and energy right out of you. You would see your life go to a new level if you dared to confront those people and start making the necessary changes.

I'm not saying it's going to be easy. If people have controlled you for a long time, they're not going to like your putting your foot down. Always do what you must in love, be kind and respectful, but stand firm and make a decision that you will live in freedom.

If you are the controller rather than the person being controlled, you, too, need to change. You're not going to be blessed by manipulating people to get your way. Quit pressuring people into doing what you want. Take the high road, walk in love, and you'll see your relationships and life become so much better.

It's liberating to understand that you don't have to keep everybody happy.

Let this be a turning point. If you have been living to please everybody else or constantly trying to fix everything, rid yourself of that false sense of responsibility. Yes, reach out to others. Yes, be kind and compassionate. But make sure you're keeping yourself happy.

Friend, if you will run your race and not let people control you and manipulate you, you'll not only have less stress and more time and energy, but I also believe you'll be happier, and you will be free to fulfill the best plan that God has for you.

Today's Prayer to Become a Better You

Continually trusting and obeying You, Father, will keep me from making myself a higher priority than You in my life. I know it's crucial to get this right.

Today's Thought to Become a Better You

Ultimately, no human being can control or manipulate me because my life belongs to God.

PART FIVE

EMBRACE THE PLACE
WHERE YOU ARE

BLOOM WHERE YOU'RE PLANTED

Be still, and know that I am God! I will be honored by every nation. I will be honored throughout the world.

PSALM 46:10

D<small>O YOU KNOW</small> someone who is not happy with where he or she is in life? She is frustrated because she is not married, and her internal body clock is sounding an alarm. Or he is upset because somebody is not treating him fairly on his career path. These people are constantly worried, trying to reason things out, trying to change things that only God can change.

I believe we create much of our own unhappiness and frustration by constantly resisting and fighting against situations and circumstances occurring in our lives. We don't understand why our prayers aren't being answered, why things aren't changing sooner. "Why has this happened to me?" Consequently, we live with unrest and uneasiness on the inside.

Learn to relax and accept the place where you are. Admittedly, it may not be a great place right now. We all have things we want to see changed, things we want to happen sooner. If we really believe that God is in control and is directing our steps, then we must believe that we are exactly where we are supposed to be. We needn't be wrestling with life and resisting our circumstances all the time.

Yes, we should resist the Enemy; we should resist sickness and other robbers of joy. But that doesn't mean that every minute we must be fighting and struggling. Some people seem to wear themselves out, constantly praying, resisting, and rebuking. They beg, "Please, God, you've got to change this situation. Change my husband. I don't like my job. My child won't do right."

No, turn all of that over to God. Your attitude should be, "God, I'm trusting You. I know that You are in control of my life. I may not understand everything that is happening, but I believe You have my best interests at heart. I'm not going to go around resisting and struggling. I'm going to relax and enjoy my life." Friend, if you can sincerely pray such a prayer, it can take an enormous amount of pressure off you.

No matter where you are, you accept it as the place God wants you to be.

The Bible says to "Be still, and know that I am God!" (Psalm 46:10). Notice you need to get still. You need to be at peace with where you are right now. Things may not be perfect. You may have some areas in which you need to improve. But as long as you are living with worry and stress, you are tying the hands of Almighty God. If you could get to a place of peace, God could fight your battles for you. He can turn your negative situations around and use them for good.

Scripture records, "Those who have believed enter the rest of God" (see Hebrews 4:3). Being in God's rest means that although you may have a problem, you trust Him to take care of it. It means that you may have a situation that you don't understand, but you are not constantly trying to figure it out. It means you have a dream in your heart, but you are not in a hurry, you're not frustrated because it hasn't come to fruition yet. In other words, when you are really in God's rest, you know that God has you in the palm of His hand. No matter where you are, you accept it as the place God wants you to be.

I'm not saying that God wants you to stay there, but if you are truly trusting Him, if you believe He is in control, then wherever you are—in either good circumstances or bad—that is where you are supposed to be. Maybe something unfair has happened; maybe somebody is not treating you right, or you are struggling financially. Still, that doesn't give you the right to live upset and frustrated.

We have to understand that God has promised He will use whatever comes into our lives for our good. He will use that difficulty to do a work in you. What you are facing currently may not be good, but if you'll keep the right attitude, He'll use it for your good.

❧ Today's Prayer to Become a Better You ❧

Father, I want to make a special point today of being still and knowing You are God. Let me relax in Your care, remembering that nothing I face is too great for You to handle.

❧ Today's Thought to Become a Better You ❧

I am exactly where God wants me to be at this moment.

LIVING ABOVE CIRCUMSTANCES

There was a young Hebrew man with us in the prison who was a slave of the captain of the guard. We told him our dreams, and he told us what each of our dreams meant.

Genesis 41:12

Circumstances can be intimidating. You may be saying, "Joel, you don't understand. I'm doing the right thing, but the wrong things are happening to me," or, "I'm in a lousy marriage," or, "People aren't treating me right."

Please don't use those attitudes as excuses to live your life in the doldrums or in the pits. Consider the Old Testament character Joseph. He spent thirteen years in prison charged with a crime he didn't commit. He could have constantly fought that injustice. He could have spent all his time trying to figure out why the horrific events happened to him. He could have easily lived his life upset, negative, and bitter, but he didn't. He simply embraced the place where he was and made the best of a bad situation. His attitude was "God, this is where You have me right now. I may not like it. I may not understand it. I don't think it's fair, but I'm not dwelling on any of that. I'm going to keep doing my best, knowing that in the end, You are going to use this to my advantage."

That's exactly what God did for him. God will do the same thing for you if you will keep your attitude positively focused on Him.

You may be frustrated because you are not yet married and think you're not going to be happy until you find a mate. Instead, relax and enjoy the place where God has you right now. Being frustrated will not make it happen any sooner, and perpetually fretting about your marital status may slow down the process of finding your mate. You have already expressed your desire to God. Why don't you just relax and say, "God, not my will but Yours be done. I'm turning this over to You. I believe You have my best interests at heart."

> The fact is, we don't grow nearly as much when everything is easy.

It is okay to be honest and pray, "God, you know I'd like to see it happen today. But I'm going to trust You and believe that at the right time, You are going to bring the right person into my life." That's what it means to trust God. You can quit trying to figure it all out on your own.

One of my favorite Scripture verses is Romans 8:28: "All things work together for good to those who love God." If you can stay in an attitude of faith, God will cause every situation to work for your good.

"Well, Joel, these people at work aren't treating me right. I'm uncomfortable. I don't like it. I want to get out of this situation."

No, we can't pray away everything uncomfortable in our lives. God is not going to remove every difficulty from you instantly. He uses those things to refine us, to do a fresh work in us. In the tough times, God develops our character. The fact is, we don't grow nearly as much when everything is easy; we grow when life is difficult, when we are exercising our spiritual muscles in the pressure spots.

Of course, none of us enjoys being uncomfortable, but it will help you to press through difficult times if you can remember that God is going to bring some good out of your discomfort. You will come out of that situation stronger than before, and God is getting you prepared for greater things.

But you have to pass the test. If you are dragging around worried, trying to figure everything out, and fighting against everything that's not going your way, you will simply prolong the process. You must recognize you are where you are for a reason. It may be because of your choices, or maybe it is merely an attack of the Enemy. Whatever it is, God will not allow anything to come into your life unless He has a purpose for it. You may not like it; you may be uncomfortable. But if you'll keep the right attitude, in the end you will come out stronger and better off than you were before.

⤫ Today's Prayer to Become a Better You ⤬

Joseph is an amazing example, Father, of someone who lived above his circumstances. Help me imitate his style more closely, leaving the details of life in Your hands.

⤫ Today's Thought to Become a Better You ⤬

Life isn't ultimately about my will but about God's will.

UNANSWERED PRAYER

SCRIPTURE READING TO BECOME A BETTER YOU   Daniel 3:1–30

If we are thrown into the blazing furnace, the God whom we serve is able to save us. He will rescue us from your power, Your Majesty. But even if he doesn't, we want to make it clear to you, Your Majesty, that we will never serve your gods or worship the gold statue you have set up.

DANIEL 3:17–18

SOME THINGS, like unanswered prayers, you may never understand this side of heaven. If you are always trying to figure them out, they will only bring frustration and confusion. Learn to trust God, and know that as long as you're doing your best, as long as you're keeping your heart pure before God, you are exactly where you're supposed to be. It may not be easy, but in the end, God is going to use it to your advantage.

One of the most important aspects of faith is trusting God even when we don't understand. A good friend of mine contracted cancer. I called him to encourage him, and I thought he'd be all down and depressed, but I was pleasantly surprised. He said, "Joel, I'm at peace. I don't like this, but I know God is still in control. And I believe in my heart that He's going to bring me through this thing."

Even in your times of greatest difficulty, even if the bottom falls out, you don't have to be distraught and let yourself get all worked up. Sometimes we think we always must be praying, resisting, quoting the Scriptures every minute. Certainly, there's nothing wrong with that. But remaining at rest, remaining in peace, keeping your joy, keeping a smile on your face, that's all part of fighting the good fight of faith as well.

If you're in a hard place, be encouraged in knowing that God is still in control of your life. He made your body. He knows your circumstances. Don't sit around depressed and discouraged. Your attitude should be, "God, I'm trusting You. I know You can do what humans can't do, and I'm committing my life into Your hands."

God, I'm going to trust You if I get my way or if I don't.

That attitude of faith pleases God. People who have made-up minds, people who say, "God, I'm going to trust You if I get my way or if I don't get my way. I will trust You in the good times and the tough times"—these are people of faith.

Recall those three Hebrew teenagers in the Old Testament who wouldn't bow down to King Nebuchadnezzar's golden idol. The king got so upset that he ordered them thrown into a fiery furnace.

The Hebrew boys said, "King, we're not worried about it. We know that our God will deliver us. *But even if He doesn't,* we're still not going to bow down." Notice, they embraced the place where they were, even though it was difficult, even though they didn't like it.

You can do something similar. Quit living frustrated because your prayers weren't answered the way you wanted. Quit being depressed because you're not as far in your career as you had hoped, or because you have a problem in your marriage or in your finances. No, just keep pressing forward. Keep your joy and enthusiasm. You may not be exactly where you hoped to be, but know this: God is still in control of your life. Moreover, as long as you keep passing the tests, no forces of darkness can keep you from fulfilling your God-given destiny.

You can have that heavy burden lifted off you. You don't have to fight and struggle all the time, trying to change everybody and everything. No, just embrace the place where you are, and believe that God is in control. He's doing a work in you. He's guiding and directing you.

If you are currently in a storm, or if you are facing some severe difficulties, hear God speaking to your heart these words: *Rise above it. Quit fighting. Quit trying to change things that only I can change.*

Believe that God has a great plan for your life. Friend, if you'll learn to embrace the place where you are, you can rise higher. You'll overcome every obstacle, and you can live that life of victory that God has in store for you!

❧ Today's Prayer to Become a Better You ❧

Father, I'm trusting You. I'm going to trust You if I get my way or if I don't get my way. I will trust You in the good times and the tough times.

❧ Today's Thought to Become a Better You ❧

Don't worry about the things that only God can change.

SOUL WELLNESS

Scripture Reading to Become a Better You   Colossians 1:3–13

We also pray that you will be strengthened with all his glorious power so you will have all the endurance and patience you need. May you be filled with joy.
Colossians 1:11

Have you ever noticed that it is in the difficult times that we grow stronger? That's when we are being stretched. That's when God is developing our character and preparing us for promotion.

We may not like it; stretching can sometimes be uncomfortable. But if we can keep the right attitude, we will come out better than we were before.

The key to passing the test is to remain in peace, at rest. When you're in peace, you have power. When you're at rest, God can fight your battles for you. Many people wear themselves out, frustrated because they don't have the job they want, upset because a child won't do right, worried over a health problem. No, turn all that over to God and be willing to go through tough times with a good attitude.

In Colossians, chapter 1, Paul prayed that the people would have the strength to endure whatever came their way. Think about that. The great apostle Paul didn't pray that God would remove every difficulty. He didn't pray that God would deliver them instantly. He prayed that they'd have the strength to go through it.

Sometimes we pray, "God, you've got to get me out of this situation today. I can't stand it any longer. If it goes on another week, I'm not going to make it." But a better way to pray is, "Father, please give me the strength to go through this with a good attitude. Help me to keep my joy. Help me to keep my peace." Our circumstances are not going to change until we change.

But you may say, "It is so difficult. I have a serious health problem. And I have this situation at work . . ." No, you have the power of the Most High God on the inside of you. You can withstand anything that comes your way. You are more than a conqueror, a victor and not a victim. Sure, we'd all love God to deliver us instantly. Most of the

Consider this: God wants you to remain at rest, to keep your peace of mind.

time, though, that's not the way He works. Make a decision to turn the situation over to God, and then stop worrying about it. Don't allow it to dominate your thoughts and words; instead, move to that place of peace and rest. Even though the situation may be hard, and you may not like it, you are growing.

God has a plan and a purpose for everything. We may not be able to see it right now. But God has promised He will not allow anything to come into our lives unless He can ultimately get some good out of it. This should take all the pressure off us. That means if our prayers aren't being answered in the way we want, God must have something better in store. He knows what's best, so you can believe that all things are going to work together for your good. Don't live stressed out when the pressure times come.

Determine in your heart and mind, *I'm not going to be depressed because my business hasn't grown as I wanted it to. Or, I refuse to lose heart merely because my child is not doing right. No, I'm going to stay in peace, trusting God, knowing that at the right time, God is going to turn it around and use it to my advantage.* That's an incredibly liberating way to live.

You may suffer from stomach problems, headaches, ulcers, and all sorts of other ailments; possibly, you can't sleep well at night because your mind is perpetually rerunning images of you fighting against everything that isn't going your way. You're trying to change things that only God can change. When God is not moving in the situation, either it is not the right time, or He is doing a work in you. Center your mind in that place of peace where you can truly say, "All right, Father, not my will but Yours."

When you understand this principle, it makes life so much easier. You won't live frustrated because your plans didn't work out. You don't have to be disappointed for a month because you didn't get the promotion you wanted. You don't have to get upset because somebody is being unfair to you. You know that God is in control and has you exactly where He wants you. As long as you keep trusting Him, God is going to fight your battles for you. That's what it says in the book of Exodus, chapter 14. "If you will remain at rest and hold your peace, then the battle is not yours, but the battle is the LORD's."

Consider this: God wants you to remain at rest, to keep your peace of mind. As long as we're upset, frustrated, and all bent out of shape, God will back away and wait. To show God that we are trusting Him, we must stay in peace; keep a smile on your face; have a good attitude day in and day out. When you are consistent, when you're stable, and when you're not moved by your circumstances, you are proclaiming, "I believe that God is in complete control of my life."

✤ Today's Prayer to Become a Better You ✤

Father, I'm placing my difficult circumstances in Your hands. I'm going to stay in peace, trusting You, knowing that at the right time, You will turn things around and use them to my advantage.

✤ Today's Thought to Become a Better You ✤

I believe that God is in complete control of my life.

CASTING BURDENS

Give your burdens to the LORD, and he will take care of you. He will not permit the godly to slip and fall.

Psalm 55:22

SOMETIMES WE CAN GET so consumed with our dreams or overcoming an obstacle that it's all we think about, talk about, and pray about, and we're not going to be happy unless it comes to pass exactly the way we want it to. That leads to frustration and, if we're not careful, possibly to resentment. When you sense that happening, you must get back to that place of rest and peace where you can honestly say, "God, I trust You. I believe that You know what's best for me. And, God, even if this doesn't work out the way I want, I'm not going to be unhappy. I'm not going to let this ruin the rest of my life. I'm making a decision that I'm going to be content right where You have me today."

One of my favorite stories in church history is that of Horatio G. Spafford, a wealthy lawyer and businessman who lived back in the 1800s. Spafford's story is not the success story, however, that we seek nowadays. In fact, he encountered horrendous tragedy in his life. His wife and four daughters were on a ship crossing the Atlantic Ocean when the vessel collided with another ship, and all four Spafford daughters lost their lives along with more than two hundred other people. Spafford's wife sent a telegram informing her husband of the terrible news.

Horatio Spafford booked passage across the Atlantic Ocean to be reunited with his grieving wife. At one point, the captain notified him that they were passing the spot where he believed Spafford's daughters had died. Horatio Spafford stared solemnly at the rolling waves, and that night he wrote the words to what would become a beloved hymn of the Christian faith: "It Is Well with My Soul."

> You can decide right now that you will trust Him wherever you are.

> When peace, like a river, attendeth my way,
> when sorrows like sea billows roll;
> whatever my lot, Thou has taught me to say,
> It is well, it is well, with my soul.

No matter what comes our way in life, we need to be able to say, "It is well with my soul. Life may have thrown me some curves, but it is well with my soul. All my dreams may not have come to pass just yet, but that's okay. I'm not in a hurry. I know in God's timing they will.

"My plans didn't work out. But nonetheless, it is well with my soul. I received a bad report from the doctor, things don't look good. But I know God has another report. I know He can do what humans can't do. And whatever happens to me, it is well, it is well with my soul." That's the kind of attitude we need to have.

You may need to get a new perspective. Perhaps you have been too focused on what you don't have, what you can't do, and what's wrong in your life. Maybe you've been telling God every five minutes what to do and how to do it, and letting Him know that you are not going to be happy unless it turns out exactly like you want it.

Make a decision to turn it over to God. Psalm 55:22 says: "Cast your burdens on the LORD. Release the weight of them and God will sustain you." No matter how dark and gloomy it looks in your life right now, if you can release the weight of those burdens, you will rise higher, and you will see the sun break forth in your life.

This starts by believing that God is in control. You can decide right now that you will trust Him wherever you are. When you do that, the battle is not yours; the battle is the Lord's. Ask God to give you the strength to endure. And rest assured He will take care of you even in the midst of life's most vicious storms.

❧ Today's Prayer to Become a Better You ❧

Father, I know that when I cast my burden on You, it is well with my soul. You lift the weight. I'm trusting You to sustain me whatever comes today.

❧ Today's Thought to Become a Better You ❧

I'm going to be content right where God has me today.

ABIDING PEACE

Scripture Reading to Become a Better You   Luke 8:22–25

As they sailed across, Jesus settled down for a nap. But soon a fierce storm came down on the lake. The boat was filling with water, and they were in real danger.

LUKE 8:23

Dᴵᴅ ʏᴏᴜ ᴋɴᴏᴡ that you can have peace even in the midst of difficult circumstances? Many people are trying to get rid of their problems, hoping they will then be happy and can then start enjoying their lives. But God wants us to learn to have peace in the midst of the storms. He wants us to have peace even when things aren't going our way—when your boss isn't treating you right, you didn't get the promotion you wanted, your child isn't doing what he should. If we make the mistake of basing our peace on our circumstances, we'll never experience God's best, because something will always upset us. You're never going to get rid of life's little aggravations. You will never get to a point where you don't have challenges or opportunities to get discouraged. We have to change our approach to life.

Jesus was asleep on a small boat when suddenly a huge storm arose. The winds were fierce and strong, batting the boat back and forth. The disciples got all upset and were afraid. They finally said, "Jesus, please get up. We're about to perish!"

Jesus got up and simply spoke to the storm. He said, "Peace, be still." Instantly, the wind subsided, and the Sea of Galilee turned to a glassy calm. The reason Jesus was able to bring peace to that situation was because He had peace inside Himself. He was in the storm, but He didn't let the storm get in Him.

Peace is not necessarily the absence of trouble, nor is it always the absence of enemies. You can have trouble and conflict all around you on the outside yet have real peace on the inside.

You may be upset and worried about some aspect of life. Perhaps you are concerned about your finances, or there's a situation at work that is unjust

> You can be
> in the storm,
> but don't let the storm
> get in you.

or unfair, and you are letting that situation rile you on the inside. Day after day it weighs on you, draining your joy, your energy, and your enthusiasm. You have let the storm get on the inside, and you need to make some changes.

"As soon as I get through this, then I'm going to get back to being my normal self," you may be saying.

No, you know that when this challenge is over, there will be something else that can steal your peace. You've got to change your approach and stop allowing those things to upset you. Instead, turn that situation over to God.

Understand that until you get to this place of peace, God can't really work in your life the way He wants to, because God works where there is an attitude of faith and expectancy, not attitudes of unbelief, worry, despair, and discouragement. Every day you will have opportunities to lose your peace. Somebody may be rude to you on the phone. You want to jump right down his throat. Instead, say to yourself, *No, I'm going to stay at peace. I'm not going to allow him to upset me.*

Or perhaps your boss doesn't give you the credit you deserve.

You didn't get the big promotion for which you were hoping. Say something to yourself such as, *That's okay. I know God is in control. I know God has something better in store for me.*

"Well, I'm upset because this man walked out of our relationship," Suzanne says. "It was wrong. It was just so unfair. I want to call him up and let him have a piece of my mind."

"No, hold your peace," I advised. "If you'll stay calm and at rest, God will bring somebody better into your life. He'll take what the Enemy meant for evil and turn it all around and use it for your advantage.

"But you've got to do your part and hold your peace. Don't live life upset, worried, and frustrated."

Sometimes we lose our peace over things we can't change. You can't change the traffic in the morning. You might as well just stay calm. You can't make your spouse or your boss or your neighbor do what's right. Only God can. You might as well enjoy your life while God is in the process of changing things in the lives of people around you.

Today's Prayer to Become a Better You

Thank You for always being in the boat with me, Father, even when I think You've fallen asleep. Help me keep my eyes and trust fixed on You rather than my circumstances when the storms come.

Today's Thought to Become a Better You

My faith will allow me to remain calm in the midst of storms.

FLY LIKE AN EAGLE

Those who trust in the LORD will find new strength.
They will soar high on wings like eagles. They will run
and not grow weary. They will walk and not faint.

ISAIAH 40:31

THROUGHOUT SCRIPTURE, the person who truly trusts in God is compared to an eagle. The eagle has some pests, one of which is the crow. He's always squawking, always causing the eagle trouble. The truth is, we all have a few crows in our lives. You may have an entire flock of them, along with a few chickens and turkeys as well!

Certain people can rub us the wrong way; they can irritate us if we allow them to. We need to take a lesson from the eagle instead. When the eagle is out flying, often a crow will come up right behind him and start to pester him, aggravating and annoying him. Although the eagle is much larger, it cannot maneuver quickly. To get rid of his pest, the eagle simply stretches out his eight-foot wingspan, catches some of the thermal currents, and rises up higher and higher. Eventually he gets to an altitude where no other bird can fly. The crow can't even breathe up there. On rare occasions, eagles have been spotted at altitudes as high as twenty thousand feet, nearly as high as a jet flies.

In the same manner, if you want to get rid of your pest, you need to rise higher. Don't ever sink down to the opposition's level. Don't argue; don't try to pay somebody back; don't give the pest the cold shoulder. Be the bigger person. Overlook faults. Walk in love, and dare to bless even your enemies. In the long run, crows can't compete with eagles.

Friend, you are an eagle. You've been made in the image of Almighty God. Learn to live above your circumstances. Rise above the petty politics at the office. Don't let people pull you into strife and division and get you all upset or gossiping.

If you want to get rid of your pest, you need to rise higher.

Always remember, the turkeys, chickens, and crows cannot live at the altitude at which you were designed to soar. God is in complete control of your life. He's promised if you will remain at rest, He'll make your wrongs right. He'll bring justice into your life. You don't have to worry, nor must you be controlled by your circumstances. You can do as the eagle and rise up above.

You won't see an eagle pecking around in the chicken coop with a bunch of chickens. An eagle lives in the high places, where he's close to God.

Moreover, when the storms come, an eagle doesn't simply go through the storm. No, he puts his wings out, catches a little more wind, and rises above it. He'll rise higher until he's completely above all that turmoil. That eagle is not concerned about the storm he's facing. He doesn't get upset. He knows he has a way out.

No doubt, he probably could fight his way through the storm, struggle and strain, and come out weary, worn, and all beat up. What a shame for him to live that way when God has given him the ability to rise above it.

Yet struggle is what many of us do. God has given us His peace. He's told us to cast our cares on Him. He said if we'll just remain at rest, He will fight our battles for us. Too often, though, we allow ourselves to become worried and upset. We let people steal our joy. We get bent out of shape if our plans don't work out exactly as we had hoped. Or maybe we're frustrated because our boss or our husband or wife is not doing what we want them to do.

You may not be able to change certain aspects of your life, but you can rise above them. Turn those situations over to God. Make a decision today that you are not going to allow those things to upset you and bother you anymore.

Did you know that the crow has to flap his wings tenaciously simply to fly? He has to work constantly. The chicken can barely get off the ground; no matter how much he flaps his wings, he's not going far. Yet an eagle merely catches the right wind currents, and he'll soar. He doesn't have to be like the crow, working and straining all the time. He just puts his wings out and rests in what God has given him, letting the winds carry him.

If you are always frustrated, trying to fix everything in your life, trying to straighten this person out for what he or she said about you, worried about your health, worried about your finances, you're acting like that crow. You're working and working, flapping and flapping. Friend, life doesn't have to be that way. Why don't you relax? God is in complete control of your life. He said He'd never leave you or forsake you. He said He'd be the friend that sticks closer than a brother.

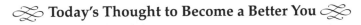

❧ Today's Prayer to Become a Better You ❧

How easily I forget, Father, that trusting You isn't about flapping harder but about letting You lift me. Thank You for Your promise not to let me fall.

❧ Today's Thought to Become a Better You ❧

To fly like an eagle, I've got to think and trust like an eagle.

PRICELESS MEMORIES

SCRIPTURE READING TO BECOME A BETTER YOU   Joshua 4:1–22

Joshua said to the Israelites, "In the future your children will ask, 'What do these stones mean?' Then you can tell them, 'This is where the Israelites crossed the Jordan on dry ground.' "

JOSHUA 4:21–22

THE PSALMIST SAID, "I recall the many miracles God has done for me. They are constantly in my thoughts. I cannot stop thinking about them." Notice, he said thoughts of God's goodness were constantly in his mind. That's a great way to live!

Too often, though, we remember what we should forget—our disappointments, hurts, and failures—and we forget what we should remember—our victories, successes, and the good times.

In the Old Testament, God commanded His people to celebrate certain feasts so they would not forget what He had done for them, and so they could pass on those inspiring stories to the next generation. Several times a year, the Israelites stopped whatever they were doing, and everybody celebrated how God brought them out of slavery, or how God defeated this or that enemy, or how He protected them against some calamity. These celebrations were not optional; they were commanded, and the people were required to attend and remember God's goodness to them.

In other places, the Bible records how God's people put down "memorial stones." These large markers were to remind the people of specific victories God had given them. Every time they or future generations passed by a memorial, they would remember the mighty things God had done. We need to do something similar. Take time to remember your victories, and celebrate what God has done in your life. Put out some memorial stones.

This is one of the best ways to build your faith and keep yourself encouraged. Remember the time that God made a way for you when it looked as if there was no way. Remember when you were so lonely, and God brought somebody special into your life. Recall

Too often we remember what we should forget . . . and we forget what we should remember.

how God has healed you or someone you know; think of how He protected you in the storm, guided you, blessed you. If you will get this awareness of God's goodness down on the inside, you won't go around thinking, *Well, I wonder if I'll ever get out of this mess? I wonder if God's ever going to work in my life.*

No, you'll be thinking, *I know if God did it for me once, He'll do it for me again!*

It would do you good to review God's goodness to you on a regular basis—simply thinking about the major victories in your life, the unexpected successes, or the times when you knew that God intervened in your circumstances. Remember the days your children were born. Remember how God gave you that job. Remember when God brought that special person into your life. Remind yourself how you fell in love and got married; thank God for your spouse and your family. Remember what God has done for you.

⨯ Today's Prayer to Become a Better You ⨯

Father, I do need to remember Your faithfulness and goodness to me. I want to spend the next few minutes telling You "Thanks" as I remember Your gifts and favor in my life.

❧ Today's Thought to Become a Better You ❧

I can trust more fully when I remember what God has already done.

REMEMBER TO REMEMBER

SCRIPTURE READING TO BECOME A BETTER YOU   Psalm 143:1–12

*I remember the days of old. I ponder all your great works
and think about what you have done.*

PSALM 143:5

WHEN WE LEARN to recall the good things God has done, it helps
us to stay in an attitude of faith and to remain grateful. It's hard to
go around complaining when you are constantly thinking about how
good God has been to you. It's hard to get negative and veer off into
unbelief when you are always talking about God's blessings and
favor in your life.

Too often we forget God is the giver of all good things. God is the
one who caused us to get that "lucky break." He's the one who
caused us to be at the right place at the right time. How many
times have you been driving on a busy highway and you said to
yourself, *Whew! That car almost hit me. Another split second and I
would have had an accident.* That was God's hand of protection.
Understand that there's no such thing as a coincidence when your life
is directed by God. When something good happens to you, be sensitive, recognize the work of God, and learn to recall it often.

I know if it were not for the goodness of God, I would not be here
today. But God showed up and made a way when it looked like
there was no way. Each of those times has become a "memorial
stone," and I don't take them for granted; I remember the great
things God has done in my life, and I thank Him for them.

I encourage you to keep a notebook, something like a diary or a journal. When something happens in your life that you know is of God, write it down. You know God opened up a door. Add that to your list. You know God spared your life, or you know God spoke to you a specific word of direction; make a note of that too. You were down and discouraged, ready to give up, when God quickened a scripture to your heart that lifted your spirits. Write that down. Keep a running record of the good things that God has done for you.

There's no such thing as a coincidence when your life is directed by God.

It need not always be something big; to others it may seem quite insignificant. But you know it is God guiding your life. You may unexpectedly meet somebody who introduces you to another person, and that leads to your getting a new client. Write that down. Maybe you are driving down the highway, and you see a new billboard that sparks an idea that you take to the office. The bosses like it, and your idea leads to a promotion. Recognize that is God at work in your life. Write that down.

Then on a regular basis, get that notebook out and read about all the great things God has done in your life. You will be encouraged! When you recall how God opened up this door for you, protected you over here, restored you there, healed you there, your faith will increase. Especially in times of difficulty, when you are tempted to get discouraged, get that notebook out and read it again. If you do that, you will not go through the day discouraged and defeated. You will know that God is in control of your life. He is holding you in the palm of His hand, and He will take care of you.

Today's Prayer to Become a Better You

Father, I realize I need to have a ready list of several memorial stones I can bring up any time I'm faced with discouragement or disappointment—those are the times when I want to remember how faithful You have already been!

❦ Today's Thought to Become a Better You ❦

What are the memorial standing stones in my life that point to God?

THE ONE IN CONTROL

Scripture Reading to Become a Better You   Philippians 2:12–18

God is working in you, giving you the desire and the power to do what pleases him.

Philippians 2:13

To truly become a better you, it is imperative to believe that God is in control of your life. Too many people go around worried and upset. They're always trying to figure everything out. How am I going to get out of this problem? How can I change my child? When am I ever going to get married? Why won't my dreams come to pass?

But that's not the way God wants us to live. When we truly trust Him and believe that He's in control, we can rest. There's a peace in our hearts and minds. Deep down on the inside, we know that everything is going to be all right.

Many times, the reason we lose our peace and begin to worry is because we don't see anything happening in the areas we are praying about or the things we are believing Him for. Everything looks the same month after month, year after year. But we have to understand that God is working behind the scenes in our lives. He has already prearranged a bright future for you. And if the curtain were pulled back so you could peer into the unseen realm, you would see God fighting your battles for you. You'd find your heavenly Father getting everything arranged in your favor. You'd see how God is getting ready to open a door and bring an opportunity across your path. I'm convinced that if we could really see how God is orchestrating everything behind the scenes, we wouldn't worry. We wouldn't live stressed-out lives.

The fact is, we all have difficulties; we all have things in life that can steal our joy, steal our peace. We have to learn to turn them over to God and say, "Father, I'm trusting You. I believe that You are in control. And even though I may not see anything tangible happening, I believe You are working in my life, going before me, making my crooked places straight, and causing me to be at the right place at the right time."

God is constantly working behind the scenes in our lives.

You may be trying to figure everything out, trying to solve every problem. But it would take so much pressure off you, and you would enjoy your life so much more, if you could just learn to relinquish control and start believing that God really is directing your steps.

The Bible reminds us, "For it is God who is all the while at work in you." Notice, God doesn't work for a while, then go off on a two- or three-year vacation, and then come back and work a little more. God is constantly at work in your life. That means that although you may not be able to see it, God is arranging things in your favor. He is getting the right people lined up to come across your path. He is looking years down the road and getting everything perfectly in order, lining up solutions to problems you haven't even considered yet. He has the right spouse for you and the right spouse for your child. He has the best opportunities, the best doors He plans to open for you. God is constantly working behind the scenes in our lives.

"Well," you say, "Joel, I've been praying for my child for two years, but I don't see anything happening," or, "I've been believing for my finances to improve, but they continue to dwindle," or, "I've been praying for the right person to come into my life, but it's been four years."

No, you don't know what God is doing behind the scenes. Don't get discouraged just because you don't see anything happening. That doesn't mean God is not working. In fact, many times God works most when we see it the least.

When we're in one of those dry seasons and we don't see anything happening, that is simply a test of our faith. We have to dig in our heels and show God what we're made of. A lot of people get negative and discouraged. "Well, I never get any good breaks. I knew nothing good would ever happen to me." "I knew I'd never get out of this problem."

No, you've got to zip that up. If you want to pass the test, you need to put a smile on your face and say, "I may not see anything happening, but I know God is working in my life."

"My child may not be doing right, but I know it's only a matter of time. As for me and my house, we will serve the Lord."

"My finances may look the same, but I'm not worried about it, I know I am blessed. I cannot be cursed. I know in my due season at the exact right time, things are going to change in my favor."

When we have this attitude of faith, we will see God do great things in our lives.

❧ Today's Prayer to Become a Better You ❧

Father, I believe that You are in control. And even though I may not see anything tangible happening, I believe You are working in my life, going before me, making my crooked places straight, and causing me to be at the right place at the right time.

❧ Today's Thought to Become a Better You ❧

As for me and my house, we will serve the Lord.

BEHIND THE SCENES

SCRIPTURE READING TO BECOME A BETTER YOU   Psalm 121:1–8

*The LORD keeps watch over you as you come and go,
both now and forever.*

PSALM 121:8

UNDERSTAND THAT the Creator of the universe is working in your life. You may be doing the same thing you've done month after month, year after year, but then all of a sudden, you bump into a person who offers you a new position; you get one idea that takes you to a new level. You are at the right place at the right time, and you meet the man or woman of your dreams. God could have been working on that ten years earlier, getting everything lined up, and then suddenly it all comes together. Suddenly your due season shows up.

Here, years and years before, you could have thought, *Nothing's happening in my life. I'll probably never get out of this problem.* Yet, the whole time, God was at work. Things were happening behind the scenes.

I'm asking you to not fall into that trap of dragging through life with no joy, no enthusiasm, and thinking nothing good is happening. You've got to shake that off and start believing that right now—not two weeks from now, but right now—God is working in your life. Right now, God is arranging things in your favor. Right now, God is fighting your battles for you. Right now, God is making your crooked places straight. And you may not see it come to pass today, but here's the key: Every day you live with faith and expectancy brings you one day closer to seeing it come to pass. If it doesn't happen today, your attitude should be, "No big deal. I know it may happen tomorrow. If it doesn't happen tomorrow, it may happen the next day. But whenever it does or doesn't happen, it's not going to steal my joy; I'm not going to live frustrated. I know God is in control and at the exact right time, it's going to come to pass. And in the meantime, I'm going to relax and just enjoy my life." You've got to believe God is in control. Believe God is working behind the scenes in your life.

> Right now,
> God is arranging
> things in your favor.

Scripture says, "God is effectually at work in those who believe" (see 1 Thessalonians 2:13). Notice that His power is activated only when we believe. God can work on your behalf your whole lifetime, and you never really get the full benefit of it because you didn't believe. Sure, you may get a break here or there, but when you really believe, when you really get up every day expecting good things, you're going to see more of God's favor. You're going to see what He's been doing behind the scenes.

✑ Today's Prayer to Become a Better You ✑

Father, thank You for an abundant life! Thank You that I can relax because You are in control. Thank You that I will never reach the end of Your surprises or faithfulness.

✑ Today's Thought to Become a Better You ✑

Every day that I live with faith and expectancy brings me one day closer to seeing God's favor come to pass.

DARING TO TRUST

SCRIPTURE READING TO BECOME A BETTER YOU   Hebrews 13:1–8

God has said, "I will never fail you. I will never abandon you."

HEBREWS 13:5

DARE TO TRUST GOD TODAY. Dare to believe that even in your disappointments, heartaches, and pains, God is right there with you. He said He would never leave you nor forsake you.

You don't have to figure everything out. You may not know what your future holds. But as long as you know who holds your future, you're going to be okay. God has been working behind the scenes in your life over the years.

I don't know what He has in store for my future, but I know I'm excited about it. It puts a spring in my step to think that the God who created heaven and earth and flung the stars into space cares so much about you and me that He is constantly working for our good. To know that God is bigger than anything you will ever face, and to know that He is already lining up answers for problems that you may not even encounter for ten or twenty years should give you incredible confidence as you enjoy your life today.

Whatever your circumstances are—whether good or bad—you need to know that God already knows about them, and He is working behind the scenes to arrange future events in your favor. Learn to trust Him. Quit worrying about it. Reject anything that hints at frustration or impatience. Remember, when you believe, you activate His power. And keep in mind that just because you don't see anything happening, that doesn't mean God is not working. Why don't you relinquish control and say, "God, I'm going to trust You. I know You have a great plan for my life."

When you believe, you activate His power.

When you do that, you will feel an enormous weight lift off you. And you'll not only enjoy your life more, but you will see more of God's blessings and favor. You will become a better you!

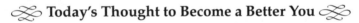

❧ Today's Prayer to Become a Better You ❧

Father, I'm going to dare to trust You in some new places. I'm going to start leaving things in Your hands that I thought I could handle. I'm going to expect good things from You.

❧ Today's Thought to Become a Better You ❧

I don't know what God has in store for my future, but I'm excited about it!

PART SIX

DEVELOP YOUR INNER LIFE

HIGHER GROUND

Scripture Reading to Become a Better You   James 4:1–10

Humble yourselves before the Lord, and he will lift you up in honor.

JAMES 4:10

Gᴏᴅ's ᴘʟᴀɴ ꜰᴏʀ ᴇᴀᴄʜ of our lives is that we continually rise to new levels. But how high we go in life, and how much of God's favor and blessings we experience, will be directly related to how well we follow His directions.

Throughout life, God will deal with us and bring areas to light where we need to improve. He often speaks to us through our conscience, or through a still, small voice. He knows the things that are holding us back. He knows our weaknesses, faults, and the inner secrets that we keep hidden. When He brings these matters to our attention, if we want continued success and blessings, we have to be willing to face the truth about ourselves and take the corrective measures God commands.

Many people don't realize the importance of dealing with such issues. Consequently, they remain stuck in ruts—a rut in their marriages or in their finances or in their careers. They casually sweep the dirt under the rug as if it doesn't matter, hoping that nobody will notice. All the while, they ignore the still, small voice.

Sometimes we think, *It's too hard to obey. I know I should forgive that person, but he hurt me so badly.* Or, *I know I need to get in*

shape, but I don't really have the time. I know I need to quit work-
ing so much, but I need the extra money.

It is important to understand that everything God tells us is for
our good. God never holds us back from His best. Nor does He pur-

**Any time you obey,
a blessing will follow.**

posely make our lives more difficult.
Quite the contrary; your heavenly
Father is waiting for your obedience so
He can release more of His favor and
blessing in your life.

Are there things in your life that God
has been dealing with you about that you have been putting off?
Maybe you keep procrastinating or ignoring His leading about getting your finances in order, being less judgmental, keeping strife out
of your home, or making peace with somebody at work. Pay attention to what God is saying to you.

Perhaps God has been dealing with you about your close friends,
the people you most frequently choose to be around. Maybe you
know some of your friends are not a good influence and are pulling
you down, but you keep making excuses. "I don't want to hurt their
feelings. Besides, if I didn't hang around them, I may not have any
other friends." But the fact is, if you will do what you know is right,
God will give you new friends. Not only that, He'll give you better
friends—people who will lift you up rather than drag you down.
Yes, you may go through a season of loneliness as you make the
transition, but I would rather be lonely for a little while, knowing
that I'm rising higher, knowing that I'm going to fulfill my destiny,
than let people pollute me and keep me from being all God created
me to be.

Anytime you obey, a blessing will follow. Why? Because you are
sowing a seed to grow and rise higher. It may not happen overnight,
but at some point, in some way, you will see God's goodness in your
life to a greater measure.

❧ Today's Prayer to Become a Better You ❧

Father, here's my life as an open book. Point out things in me that prevent me from seeing and receiving all You have for me. Help me turn from anything that doesn't please You.

❧ Today's Thought to Become a Better You ❧

In order to rise, I need to release what's holding me down.

THROUGH THE ROOF

Scripture Reading to Become a Better You   1 Kings 19:1–18

After the earthquake there was a fire, but the LORD was not in the fire. And after the fire there was the sound of a gentle whisper.

1 Kings 19:12

My questions to you are: How high do you want to rise? Do you want to continue to increase? Do you want to see more of God's blessings and favor? If so, the higher you go, the more disciplined you must be; the quicker you must obey. If you're hanging around people who compromise and cheat on their spouses and have no integrity, you're just asking for trouble.

"Well, Joel, they are good people, and their conduct doesn't affect me. It doesn't seem to hurt me one bit."

No, you don't know how much your association with them is holding you back. You don't know what God wants to release, but He cannot and will not until you get away from those negative influences. If you will do as He says, you will see God's favor in a new way, and your entire life will rise to a higher level.

Understand, the longer we delay dealing with a character issue, the more difficult it is to do later on. You'd be far better off if you'd learn to obey God's promptings quickly. The moment you feel the uneasiness, the moment an inner alarm sounds and something says, *This isn't right,* take the proper steps to move away from that action, comment, or attitude. That may well be God talking to you—trying to keep you on His best path for your life.

God has given us our own free will. He will not force us to do what is right. He won't force us to make good decisions. It's up to each one of us individually to pay attention to the still, small voice; we mustn't get so busy or self-directed that we miss what God is trying to tell us. Learn to act on His leading.

God won't force us to make good decisions.

God's directions often affect the most practical aspects of our lives. Recently, a young woman told me that she felt a strong urge to go to the doctor to get a medical checkup. She looked as healthy as could be, she was active and energetic, and she exercised regularly. Nevertheless, the feeling persisted: *Go see the doctor. Go get a checkup.* That still, small voice was speaking to her. For several weeks, she ignored it and put it off, thinking, *Oh, I'm fine. That's not a message for me.*

But she couldn't get away from it. She finally decided to schedule an appointment with her doctor. During a routine checkup, the doctor discovered a small cyst in her body and found that it was malignant. Thankfully, he was able to remove the malignancy completely, because it hadn't spread. The young woman required no further treatment. But after the operation, the doctor told her, "It's a good thing you came in when you did, because a couple of years later, this could have been a major problem, possibly even life-threatening."

The young woman was so grateful. She later told me, "Joel, I know that was God. I would not have gone to the doctor for that checkup had it not been for God's promptings."

We need to listen to the still, small voice. God knows what's best for us.

✑ Today's Prayer to Become a Better You ✑

Father, I want to have ears that hear Your voice. I realize I need to pay attention. Thank You for Your willingness to speak to me through Your Word and in my life.

✑ Today's Thought to Become a Better You ✑

Am I listening to God's still, small voice today?

BACK ON GOD'S HIGHWAY

SCRIPTURE READING TO BECOME A BETTER YOU   Psalm 51:1–19

Restore to me the joy of your salvation, and make me willing to obey you.

PSALM 51:12

YOU CAN DO a lot in life and get away with it. You can run with the wrong crowd and still get to heaven. You can treat people disrespectfully or be sloppy in your business affairs and still live in relative comfort. But I'm talking about rising higher. I'm talking about being the very best you can be.

Many people wonder why they're not happy, why they are not blessed and increasing in influence, why they can't sleep well at night. Often it is because their consciences are not clear. We cannot bury things in our subconscious minds and expect to rise higher and enjoy God's best.

When King David committed adultery with Bathsheba, he tried to cover it up. Making matters worse, he sent Bathsheba's husband, Uriah, to the front lines of the battle and then ordered his general to pull back, resulting in Uriah's certain death. For one full year, David pretended that everything was okay; he went on with life and business. No doubt, he thought, *If I don't deal with it, if I ignore it, it won't bother me; it won't affect me.*

That year was one of the worst of David's life. He was miserable. Scripture says he was also weak; he grew sick physically and had all kinds of problems. That is what happens when we refuse to deal with things. We step out of God's protection and favor. When we live with a guilty conscience, we don't feel good about ourselves, so we take it out on other people. Many times, just like David, we're weak, defeated, living in mediocrity. It's because of the poison on the inside.

When you do wrong, don't run away from God.

But, friend, none of us needs to live that way. Our God is a forgiving, merciful God. When you make a mistake, you don't have to hide it. When you do wrong, don't run away from God. Run *to* God.

After a year of living in denial, King David finally admitted his sin and his mistakes after a prophet confronted the king about his misdeeds. David said, "God, I'm sorry. Please forgive me. Create in me a clean heart. Restore the joy of my salvation." When David sincerely did that, God restored him. That's how David got his joy, peace, and victory back. Although he had failed miserably, he went on to do great things.

Now think about it: David could have been stuck right there in defeat, in mediocrity, for the rest of his life had he refused to deal with that issue. But he chose to change, and God helped him to do it.

Are there things in your life that you are refusing to deal with? When you ask for forgiveness, God can restore you. That's when He'll put you back on your best path. That's when He'll give you a new beginning.

Keep in mind, God deals with each of us individually. We are all at different levels, so we should never compare ourselves to others. Too often, when we compare ourselves with others, we tend to make excuses for ourselves. For instance, maybe all your friends are going to see a movie, but you read the review and don't feel good about it. You know it would not be God's best for you. Your inner alarm goes off, and your conscience cautions you, *You are better than that; don't willingly take dirt into your mind.*

Right there is an opportunity for you to rise higher. Sure, you could attempt to quiet your conscience and say, "Oh, it's not going to hurt me. I'm strong, and besides, all my friends love God. They attend church. They're good people. They're going to see that movie."

No, maybe your friends are at a different stage in their spiritual walk than you. Or perhaps they are ignoring God's voice speaking to them; maybe they would be much more blessed if they would quit giving in and living at such a low level. You must do what you feel good about in your own heart. It may cost you a few friendships. It may mean that you spend a few lonely nights. Or maybe you can't play on a team that parties after every game.

Remember that anything God asks you to do is for your benefit. It's so He can ultimately release more of His favor into your life.

Moreover, anything God asks of us, He always gives the grace to do it. If God asks you to forgive somebody, you may not think you can, but if you will take that step of faith, God's grace will be there to help you. You don't get the grace unless you step out. You have to make the first move. God will see that step of faith, and He'll give you supernatural strength to help you overcome any obstacles standing in the way of doing the right thing.

✥ Today's Prayer to Become a Better You ✥

Father, I know You are the great restorer. As You did for David, You have done for me. Help me to continually run to you each time I fail. You are my hope.

✥ Today's Thought to Become a Better You ✥

God will give me grace to do what He wants me to do.

A TENDER CONSCIENCE

Cling to your faith in Christ, and keep your conscience clear. For some people have deliberately violated their consciences; as a result, their faith has been shipwrecked.
                                                              1 TIMOTHY 1:19

YOUR CONSCIENCE is often called the compass of the soul. It works like an inward monitor, similar to an alarm. When you're about to do something that is not beneficial or something that will get you into trouble, your conscience causes you to feel uneasy. Don't ignore that warning. That's your conscience helping you to know what is right and what is wrong. One of the best friends you can ever have is your own conscience.

We could avoid a great deal of trouble and heartache if we would maintain a more tender conscience. I hear people say all the time, "I know I shouldn't do this, but . . ." or "I know I shouldn't say this, but . . ." or "I know I shouldn't buy this, but . . ."

They know what they should do. The alarm is going off. They can feel that sense of disapproval, but they choose to disobey their own conscience. Someday they will look back and recognize how God tried to warn them again and again.

Don't make the mistake of overriding your conscience. Respect it. Just as you respect your boss or someone else with authority over you, learn to treat your conscience in the same way. God will use your conscience to help lead you and keep you out of trouble. Perhaps you are in a conversation with your spouse, and things are heating up. You can feel yourself getting aggravated, wanting to continue the argument more forcefully, when suddenly that inner alarm goes off. Something down inside says, *Let it go. Drop it. Bite your tongue. Walk away. Keep the peace.*

Don't make the mistake of overriding your conscience.

That's your conscience trying to keep you out of trouble. That's God trying to warn you. Too many times we ignore it and choose to do our own thing. We end up having a big argument and getting all upset, ruining the rest of the evening. It could have been avoided if we would have paid attention to what our conscience was trying to say to us.

Learn to be sensitive. Stop when your conscience says stop. Quit having to have the last word. Pay attention to what you're feeling inside, and don't override your own conscience.

When you feel uncomfortable down inside, pull back and pay attention to what God is trying to say to you. You may be in the middle of a conversation. All of a sudden the alarm goes off, and you know you need to button your lip or walk away. Don't ignore that warning from your conscience.

You may be ready to buy something or eat something or make some less than noble plans when that inner siren goes off. If you will learn to be sensitive and listen to your conscience, God will keep you out of trouble. He will help you make good decisions. He can protect you from danger.

✑ Today's Prayer to Become a Better You ✑

Father, thank You for my conscience. It's my onboard early-warning system against dangers. Help me listen more closely to the siren. And thank You for all the ways You speak to me.

≈ **Today's Thought to Become a Better You** ≈

My conscience is one of God's message boards in my life.

THE PACE OF CHANGE

SCRIPTURE READING TO BECOME A BETTER YOU   1 Timothy 4:12–16

Give your complete attention to these matters. Throw yourself into your tasks so that everyone will see your progress.

1 TIMOTHY 4:15

UNDERSTAND THIS: When you live an obedient life, God's blessings will chase you down and overtake you. When you obey, you cannot outrun the good things of God.

God does not expect you to change overnight. He is not going to be disappointed with you or write you off if you don't turn your life around in one week's time. No, all He asks is that you keep making progress. He doesn't want you to be at this same place next year. He will lead you in His own special way, and if you will be sensitive and do your best to keep your own conscience clear, God will be pleased, and He'll release more of His blessings into your life.

God meets us at our own level. I don't have to keep up with you, and you don't have to keep up with me. I just have to be true to my own conscience. I know the areas in which God deals with me most frequently, and I do my best not to go against my own conscience. That's what I'm challenging you to do as well.

A young man with whom I attended college had a habit of being short with people. Sometimes he was downright rude. One day we were at a restaurant together with a group of guys from the school, and the waiter mixed up my friend's order. My friend jumped down the waiter's throat. I mean he let him have it and embarrassed him in front of all of us.

After we got back to the dorm, my friend came into my room about an hour later and asked if he could borrow my car. I said, "Sure you can, but where are you going at this late hour?"

"Joel, I feel terrible," he said. "I treated that waiter so badly, I can't even sleep. I'm going to go back there and apologize to him."

> When you live an obedient life, God's blessings will chase you down and overtake you.

That young man changed over the course of that year. He went from being hard, cold, and rude to being one of the kindest, most considerate people you could ever meet. God will help you to change if you will simply work with Him.

None of us is perfect. We all make mistakes, but we can learn to obey our own conscience if we can be big enough to say, "I'm sorry; I didn't treat you right; I'll do better next time." If you will be sensitive and maintain a clear conscience, there's no limit to what God will do in your life. In contrast, when you have a guilty conscience, you don't feel good about yourself. You're not happy; you can't pray with boldness; you feel condemned. You don't expect good things, and you usually don't receive them.

At that point, the best thing you can do is go back and make things right. Like that young man, swallow your pride and be quick to obey. Apologize to the people you have offended. Don't live with a guilty conscience.

Or maybe you need to say, "God, I'm sorry; please forgive me for having such a critical attitude toward that person."

When you do that, your conscience will relax. That heavy burden will be lifted off you; you'll be able to sleep well. Not only that, but God will help you do better next time.

✑ Today's Prayer to Become a Better You ✑

Father, I'm counting on You for courage to make things right when I go wrong. Use my conscience to alert me to times when I offend others, and help me be swift in my apologies. Thank You for guarding my steps.

✑ Today's Thought to Become a Better You ✑

I'm not perfect, but God is helping me make progress!

A CLEAR CONSCIENCE

SCRIPTURE READING TO BECOME A BETTER YOU   Matthew 6:19–24

Your eye is a lamp that provides light for your body. When your eye is good, your whole body is filled with light.

MATTHEW 6:22

Y EARS AGO, one time after a service, my father came back into the television production area. Four or five crew members and I were gathered there, and when my dad walked in, we were all laughing and having a good time. Something really funny had just happened. For some reason, my father thought we were making fun of someone in the service, but it didn't have anything to do with that.

Now, ordinarily, my father was a very kind and compassionate person, but this incident seemed to set him off. He began to chew us out, letting us know we should not be making fun of people, and on and on. I said, "Daddy, it had nothing to do with that; it was totally unrelated," but he didn't accept that.

He left, and, of course, the guys on the crew and I felt bad about the misunderstanding. When I got home that night a couple of hours later, my father came into my room. "Joel, I've got to talk to you," he said. "I blew it tonight. I know I was wrong. I know I made a mistake, and I'm asking you to forgive me, please. I want to apologize." Before I'd gotten home, my dad had called each of those other young men as well and apologized to them. It must have been close to midnight, but he would not go to bed with that heaviness on his heart.

What an impression that made upon me! What an impression it made upon those other young men. My father was the boss, but he was not too proud to admit that he had made a mistake and needed to apologize. See, my father had a tender conscience. No wonder God blessed him. No wonder God used him in a great way.

If we can learn to have that kind of sensitive, pure heart and be quick to obey, quick to forgive, quick to apologize, and quick to change our attitudes, we will be pleasing to God.

> **If your conscience is clear, life is good.**

Live your life with a clear conscience. Get into God's best plan. Scripture says in Matthew 6:22 that the lamp of the body is the eye. Your "spiritual eye" is your conscience. Jesus goes on to say that if the eye is clear, the whole body will be filled with light. In other words, if your conscience is clear, life is good. You're going to be happy. You will have a positive vision and will enjoy God's blessings.

Then the next verse describes many people today. It says in the Amplified Bible, "If . . . [your conscience] is darkened, how dense is that darkness!" Many people are living with a heaviness hanging over their lives. They have some nagging feeling, something's always bothering them. They're not happy. The problem is, they don't have a clear conscience. They've ignored the warnings for too long. They've gotten hard and cold in certain areas.

That insensitivity won't change until you make the proper adjustments. If there are things that you are doing that you know you should not be doing, then make some adjustments. Or if there are things that you should be doing and you're not, then make those changes. As I've said, it may not be something big. You may not be living in some sordid sin, but maybe God is dealing with you about having a better attitude, about spending more time with your children, about eating healthier. Whatever it is, make a decision that you're going to pay more attention to your conscience and that you are going to be quick to obey. That's when the heaviness will leave. I like what the apostle Paul said in Acts 23. He said, "I have always lived before God with a clear conscience."

That should be our goal as well. When our conscience is clear, condemnation flees. When we have a clear conscience, we can be happy. Other people may try to judge us or condemn us, but that negative input will bounce right off us.

Sometimes people say, "Joel, why don't you do more of this or more of that?"

I know I'm not perfect, but I also know this: My conscience is clear before God. I know that I'm doing my best to please Him. That's why I can sleep well at night. That's why I can lie down in peace. That's why I have a smile on my face. Friend, keep your conscience tender, and you will discover that life keeps getting better and better.

✺ Today's Prayer to Become a Better You ✺

Father, I want my conscience to be consistently clear before You. When it gets cloudy, I want to clear it up. Thank You for the gift of forgiveness that clears my conscience.

✺ Today's Thought to Become a Better You ✺

Sensitivity will preserve the 20/20 vision in my conscience.

ROOT ISSUES

SCRIPTURE READING TO BECOME A BETTER YOU   Hebrews 12:14–17

Look after each other so that none of you fails to receive the grace of God. Watch out that no poisonous root of bitterness grows up to trouble you, corrupting many.
                                                                    HEBREWS 12:15

TOO MANY PEOPLE never really look inside and get honest with themselves. They don't get down to the root of their problems. Instead, they simply deal with the fruit, the surface issues. They may be negative or can't get along in relationships. Perhaps they have low self-esteem, severe financial problems, or some other chronic problem. They try to improve their behavior, and that is admirable, but many times their efforts produce only temporary results because they refuse to deal with the bad root. Consequently, they continue to produce bad fruit.

The Bible teaches that we should not let a root of bitterness spring forth and contaminate our whole lives. It's like having a weed out in your front yard. You can pull that weed, but if you merely clip it off at the surface, you are not really getting down to the roots. A couple of days later, you look out in your yard, and you have that same weed to deal with again.

For lasting, positive change, you must go deeper and not merely look at what you do, but ask yourself these questions: *What is the root of this problem? Why do I act this way? Why am I out of control in this area? Why am I always so defensive? Why do I feel that*

I must repeatedly prove myself to everybody? Only as you get to the root and start dealing with the source of the problem can you realistically expect positive changes.

We need to examine carefully the areas in which we constantly struggle. Are our spouses really at fault? Is it really our circumstances, upbringing, or environment? Or could it be that we have something buried deep within that is causing us to "be infected"?

As long as they have that bad root, they're going to continue to produce the wrong kind of fruit.

This is especially important in the area of your relationships. Many people have a root of rejection—they have been through hurts in the past. Somebody did them wrong, and rather than letting it go, they hold on to it. That bitterness poisons every part of the person's life.

I know people who have a root of insecurity that causes them to feel defensive. They're always trying to prove to somebody else who they are. As long as they have that bad root, they're going to continue to produce the wrong kind of fruit.

So often we can't seem to get along with a particular person, and we're sure it must be his or her fault. We're sure it's our spouse. We're sure it's our boss or coworkers. But wait. Could the problem be you? Could it be that you have a root of pride that is causing you to withhold forgiveness or is blinding you to somebody else's opinion? We can try to correct all these things on the surface, but that's similar to merely putting a fresh bandage on an infected wound or cutting a surface weed. The problem will keep coming back until we get to the real source.

✑ Today's Prayer to Become a Better You ✑

Father, thank You for the truth that I'm not stuck dealing with symptoms of problems but that You can help me get to the root of issues. I know You will give me the strength to change.

✑ Today's Thought to Become a Better You ✑

I can do all things through Christ who strengthens me.

OPENING SEALED ROOMS

I don't want you to forget, dear brothers and sisters, about our ancestors in the wilderness long ago. All of them were guided by a cloud that moved ahead of them, and all of them walked through the sea on dry ground . . . . Yet God was not pleased with most of them, and their bodies were scattered in the wilderness.

1 CORINTHIANS 10:1, 5

WE HAVE TO UNDERSTAND that most of our problems have deeper roots. We might be amazed at how many things affect us negatively, and we are trying to solve the problem simply by dealing with the fruit—often treating surface issues for years on an endless treadmill.

The children of Israel were doing something similar. They wandered around in the wilderness between Egypt and the Promised Land of Canaan for forty years—a trip that should have been a mere eleven-day journey. The root cause of their problem was that they had developed a victim mentality. Granted, they had been treated horribly during the last portion of their time in Egypt; they had been through many painful, unfair experiences while in slavery. The inner pain followed them, even after God had miraculously delivered them from bondage. Out in the desert, they blamed Moses for their lack of food and water; they blamed the past, complained about the food, and fretted over their enemies. It never dawned on them that they were a part of the problem. Because of their lack of faith, they kept going around the same mountain year after year, never making any real progress.

Perhaps you have been stuck at the same place in your life for far too long. Maybe you are stuck in a sour marriage or a dead-end career. Or maybe you are stuck in a quagmire of debt or negative attitudes; you are often hard to get along with, defensive, or critical.

> They kept going around the same mountain year after year, never making any real progress.

It's time to get up and get going. Our prayer should be, "God, please show me the truth about myself. I don't want to be at this same place next year, so if I have things holding me back, show me what they are. Help me, Father, to change. Help me to get to the root of my problems."

God is knocking on the door of new rooms in our hearts, maybe rooms that we haven't let Him enter previously. The only way He'll come in is if we invite Him. The doorknob is on the inside. I have discovered that I can allow God in some rooms of my heart yet keep Him out of other rooms. Opening the door to these rooms can be painful or embarrassing. Hidden in some of those rooms are hurts and wounds from the past. It's where our weaknesses and shortcomings are tucked away. Rather than dealing with the issues and cleaning the crud out of those dark corners, we keep those rooms locked. We make excuses for our behavior; we blame other people. Sometimes, we even blame God.

"That's just the way I am," someone might say.

God continues to knock. If we want to get to the source, then we must look inside; we must allow God to shine the floodlight of His Word in every room of our hearts. When we have feelings that we know are wrong, rather than hiding them and trying to bury them away in one of these rooms, the best thing we can do is to be honest and ask, "God, why do I feel this way?" "Why can't I get along with my spouse?" "Why do I try to manipulate everybody?" "God, why do I always have to have my way?" "Why do I get upset so easily?" If you will be honest and willing to face the truth rather than hiding behind excuses, God will show you some answers to those questions. As you begin to act on that truth, you can come up higher.

If you're impatient, be honest enough to say, "God, show me why I'm so impatient. And then please help me to deal with it."

When you feel resentment toward another person, tending to be critical or finding fault, the first thing you should do is to pray, "Please, God, show me why I don't like this person. What's wrong on the inside of me? God, am I jealous of her position, jealous of his money, jealous of their talents? God, please show me the truth about myself. I don't want to go around that same mountain another year. I want to come up higher; I want to enter my Promised Land."

✐ Today's Prayer to Become a Better You ✐

God, please show me the truth about myself. I don't want to be at this same place next year, so if I have things holding me back, show me what they are. Help me, Father, to change. Help me to get to the root of my problems.

✐ Today's Thought to Become a Better You ✐

With God's help I can skip life's treadmill.

SET A NEW STANDARD

SCRIPTURE READING TO BECOME A BETTER YOU   Luke 9:51–62

*Jesus told him, "Anyone who puts a hand to the plow and
then looks back is not fit for the Kingdom of God."*

LUKE 9:62

DIGGING OUT DEEP-ROOTED problems can be painful. The easy
thing is to concentrate on surface issues, to maintain the status
quo. The comfortable way is to avoid change. There is a pain asso-
ciated with coming up higher. It's uncomfortable to be honest and
really deal with these issues. It can be difficult to have to forgive an
offense when it was somebody else's fault. It's hard to admit sometimes, "I'm holding on to the bitterness," or, "I'm defensive because
I'm so insecure," or, "I'm hard to get along with because I'm dragging all my baggage from the past." Moreover, don't be surprised if,
as you shed the superficial layers and really get honest, you feel a little pressure. Please understand that this discomfort is only temporary. It's a growing pain, and once you get past that point, you're
going to move up to a new level of victory. The pain of change is
much less than the pain of staying in mediocrity.

Perhaps you have been spinning your wheels, going around in cir-
cles year after year, and are not really happy. You need to be honest
enough to say, "God, show me what it is. Am I relying on other people to make me happy? Do I have unrealistic expectations? Am I
going to be happy only if I get married? Am I allowing my circumstances to keep me down? God, show me the truth about myself."

Not too long ago a man told me that whenever he took time to enjoy his life, he felt guilty about it. He felt condemned, as though he were doing something wrong. Over the years, he immersed himself in his work, not taking any time for himself, not taking any time for

The pain of change is much less than the pain of staying in mediocrity.

his family. Ironically, his overworking was all because of these feelings of guilt. His life was out of balance. This went on year after year until one day he decided to get honest and let God in that room of his heart. He said, "God, why do I feel this way? Why do I feel guilty when I just want to go out and have fun, to enjoy being with my family?"

He realized that as he was growing up, his father was extremely strict. He came from a military family, and his dad didn't allow any fun in the house. Everything was serious. He didn't really know what it was like to have a normal childhood. He was taught to work, to be serious, with little to no playtime. Now an adult himself, he realized that he had become just like his father. Those thoughts, those attitudes, those habits were what he had learned early on—not that they were right, but that's all he had known. Once he recognized what the source was, he was able to break that heaviness and really start enjoying his life.

You may have come out of an abusive situation. Maybe somebody else caused you a lot of heartache and pain; perhaps the people who raised you were unkind, or somebody with whom you shared a relationship used or abused you. They made poor decisions, and now you are dealing with the ramifications of those decisions. But please don't let that be an excuse. You can come up higher. You can set a new standard.

✤ Today's Prayer to Become a Better You ✤

Father, I'm glad I can talk to You about root issues. Please reveal to me in these quiet moments those problems You want to work on in me.

✤ Today's Thought to Become a Better You ✤

I can come up higher; I can set a new standard!

PART SEVEN

STAY PASSIONATE ABOUT LIFE

ANTICIPATING GOD'S BLESSING

Though a thousand fall at your side, though ten thousand
are dying around you, these evils will not touch you.

PSALM 91:7

IF YOU WANT to become a better you, it is important to take the right actions along with having faith. It's not enough to believe, as important as that may be. We have to take it one step further and start expecting. While we are expecting good things from God, we should be making plans. We need to talk as if what we are praying about is going to happen. We should dare to step out in faith and act like it's going to happen.

When a couple is expecting a baby, they make all sorts of preparations. Why? Because they know a child is on its way. The fact is, in the early stages of the pregnancy, they haven't seen the baby or touched it. Yet they have faith in the doctor's report, so they start making preparations.

God has put dreams in every one of our hearts. We all have things for which we are believing—perhaps you are believing to overcome an illness, believing to get out of debt, or believing to accomplish your dreams. Here's the key: We have to go beyond believing. True faith puts action behind it. If you're sick, you need to start making plans to get well. If you're struggling in your finances, start making plans to prosper. If your marriage is on the rocks, start making plans to see that relationship restored. Lay your faith on the line.

Too often, we say we are believing God for good things, yet with our actions, we're doing just the opposite. Understand that your faith will work in either direction, positively or negatively. I know some people who plan to get the flu. At the grocery store, I hear them predicting their future: "Well, it's flu season. I had better pick up some of this flu medicine just in case. After all, it was bad last year. I got lucky and didn't get it. But I'll probably get it this year." They talk as though it is sure to happen. They take it even further and put actions behind their negative faith, by purchasing the flu medicine. Not surprisingly, a few weeks later they come down with the flu. Their faith worked, albeit negatively. They expected the flu, made plans for it, and they got it. Remember, your faith will work in either direction.

**Your faith will work
in either direction.**

Please don't misinterpret what I am saying. It is prudent to take precautions; we have medicine at our house. However, I don't think we should run to the pharmacy every time a television commercial announces that flu season is here.

Funny, sometimes we put more faith in those commercials than we do in what God says. I love what it says in Psalms: "A thousand may fall at my side, ten thousand at my right hand; but it will not come near my dwelling." Everybody at work may be getting the flu, everybody at school may have it, but I believe God has put a hedge of protection around me, and I'm going to stay in faith and not make plans to get it.

If we read the news long enough and watch all the studies, they'll nearly talk us into having heart disease, high cholesterol, diabetes, and all sorts of ailments. "Well, you know what they say, one in four people gets cancer," a pessimistic friend points out.

Maybe that's true, but let's believe we will be among the three who don't get it instead of one of those who do. It is just as easy to believe for the positive as it is the negative. Start making plans to live a long healthy life. When you face sickness—and we all have things come against us from time to time—don't just give up and start making plans to live with it. I've had people tell me, "Well, Joel, I'm learning to live with my arthritis. I'm learning to live with my high blood pressure."

No, that's not your high blood pressure; that's not your sickness. Quit taking ownership of it, and start making plans to get well. Our attitude should be, "This sickness didn't come to stay, it came to pass." Say things such as, "I know with long life, God is going to satisfy me. So I declare it by faith—I'm getting better and better every day in every way."

✥ Today's Prayer to Become a Better You ✥

Father, I can sense my hopes rising. I know I am free to plan on Your blessing in the future, because that's what You have promised!

✥ Today's Thought to Become a Better You ✥

By faith I'm claiming God's blessing ahead of time.

NOW FAITH

Don't worry about tomorrow, for tomorrow will bring its own worries. Today's trouble is enough for today.
                                                            MATTHEW 6:34

Don't quit dreaming. Keep the vision in front of you. A friend of mine was in an accident where both of his knees were crushed. The doctor told him he would be fortunate to walk, but he would certainly never run or play sports again. My friend was so disappointed. After being in the hospital for over three months, the first thing he did when he was discharged was join a health club. He took a step of faith.

The fact is, he couldn't go to the club for over a year. He was too weak, but he made up his mind he was not going to sit back and plan on staying in that wheelchair; he was making plans to be up walking again. That was more than five years ago, and today that young man can outrun me. He defied the odds. What happened? He started making plans to rise up out of that injury. He could have easily let the doctor's negative words sink in, convincing him to give up and settle for mediocrity. Instead, he believed God and began making plans to be well.

Faith is always in the now.

Maybe you've had some negative things happen to you or some negative comments spoken over you. Don't allow those negatives to take root. Keep believing for good things. And remember, faith is always in the now. Get up every morning saying, "Father, I thank You that right now You are working in my life. I thank You that right now I'm getting better. Right now things are changing in my favor."

Stay in the now; faith is always in the present.

Today's Prayer to Become a Better You

Father, I thank You that right now You are working in my life. I thank You that right now I'm getting better. Right now things are changing in my favor.

Today's Thought to Become a Better You

God is intimately here with me in this moment, eager to express His love.

FAITHFUL HERITAGE

SCRIPTURE READING TO BECOME A BETTER YOU

Deuteronomy 34:1–12

Moses was 120 years old when he died, yet his eyesight was clear, and he was as strong as ever.

DEUTERONOMY 34:7

GRANDMOTHER OSTEEN, my grandmother on my father's side, was a feisty woman. She stood only about five feet tall, but she had a big faith. One time, when she was older in life, she went to see her doctor. He said, "I'm sorry, Mrs. Osteen, but you're in the beginning stages of Parkinson's disease."

Well, Grandmother Osteen didn't know what that was, but she was sure she didn't want to have any part of it. She bristled back and got real stern. She said, "Listen here, doctor, I'll not have that. I refuse to have it. I'm too old to have it."

She went home and never did come down with Parkinson's disease. She just kept doing what she'd always been doing, planning on living a long, healthy life. She didn't let the negative words take root.

I realize that we can't just wish things away; sometimes we can't even pray them away, but we can decide what we're going to plan for. We can plan to get old and lose our health, or we can plan to live a long, healthy, blessed, prosperous life.

What are you planning for today? Sickness or divine health? To barely get by or to be blessed? To stay where you are or to rise higher and accomplish your dreams? According to our actions or lack of action, we are making plans for something.

There's an interesting story in the Bible about a widow. Her husband died, and she didn't have enough money to pay her bills. The creditors were coming to take her two sons as payment. The only thing she had of any value was a small pot of oil. Elisha the prophet showed up at her home and instructed her to do something rather unusual. He said, "Go out to all your neighbors and gather up as many large empty containers as you can find, big jars that can be used to hold oil." Elisha told her specifically, "Don't get just a few; get as many as you can possibly find."

> According to our actions or lack of action, we are making plans for something.

No doubt, in the natural, it seemed like the woman was simply wasting her time. Elisha knew he had to get her faith going in the right direction. She had been sitting around long enough preparing for defeat. Now he was trying to get her to start preparing for victory. So she gathered up all sorts of empty containers and brought them home. Then Elisha told her to pour the oil that she had into one of the other containers. At first, it looked as though she was merely going to transfer it from one container to another, but Scripture says her oil never ran out. She kept pouring and pouring and pouring. God supernaturally multiplied it until every single container was completely full. If she would have gotten a dozen more containers, they would have been full as well. Friend, we are the ones who limit God; His resources are unlimited. If you will believe Him for more, regardless of your circumstances, He can provide—even if it takes a miracle to do so!

Let me challenge you: Have a big dream for your life. Make provision for abundance.

❧ Today's Prayer to Become a Better You ❧

Father, I want to expect more from You. I realize You are worthy of my highest expectations. No one can deliver like You can deliver. I'm planning on Your favor.

❧ Today's Thought to Become a Better You ❧

I'll plan on God's best, and I won't be disappointed.

MAKING MELODY

Scripture Reading to Become a Better You   Ephesians 5:15–20

Be filled with the Holy Spirit.

Ephesians 5:18

One of the secrets to becoming a better you is to keep singing the song that God has put in your heart—even if you can't carry a tune in a bucket! Let me explain. Too many people go around negative and discouraged, allowing their problems and circumstances to weigh them down. They live stressed out, dragging through each day, not really excited about life. I've had people tell me, "Joel, I've got too many problems to enjoy life," or, "The reason I'm discouraged and not happy is because I have all these things coming against me."

The fact is, God has put a well of joy on the inside of each one of us. Our circumstances may be negative; things may not be going our way. But if we can learn to tap into this joy, we can still be happy. We can live with enthusiasm in spite of what comes against us.

One of the keys is found in Ephesians 5:18. It says, "Ever be filled with the Spirit." Notice, you don't just get filled one time and then live happily ever after. Scripture says to be "ever filled." That means we can be filled on a continual basis. How can we do this?

The next verses reveal the secret: "By speaking to yourselves in psalms and hymns, by making melody in your heart, and by being grateful." In other words, the way to keep your life full of joy and the way to overcome the pressures of life is by keeping a song of praise in your heart. All through the day, we should be singing, if not aloud then at least silently allowing a song of praise to dance through our minds. You may not actually vocalize words and music. You may simply express a grateful attitude. In your thoughts, you are thinking about God's goodness. Or maybe you go around hum-

Scripture says to be "ever filled."

ming a tune. Maybe it's something as simple as whistling while you work, but throughout the day, you're making melody in your heart. Under your breath, you're saying, "Lord, thank You for this day. Thank You that I'm alive and healthy."

When you do that, you are filling up on the inside; God is replenishing your strength; He's refilling your supply of joy and peace. The very things that so often become depleted through the stress, disappointments, and rigors of the day, God wants to refresh in your life. When you keep singing that song of praise, you can be continually refilled, filling up faster than the depletion caused by life's taking a toll on you. That's how we stay full of the Spirit.

"Well, I went to church on Sunday," Mike said. "I read my Bible before I went to work. Isn't that enough?"

No, this is an ongoing process. To be ever filled means we have to get in a habit of being refilled throughout the day—especially on those tough days.

Think back to when somebody gave your child some helium-filled balloons on her birthday. For the first few days following the party, the balloons remain bright and beautiful. They fly high at the end of their strings, bobbing in the wind. If you let go, the balloons would take off into the air. In a couple of days, though, the balloons begin to shrivel and shrink, sinking down, lower, smaller, weaker. Day by day, the balloons drop lower and lower. Finally, they land on the floor, totally deflated. The balloons have lost their life and attractiveness, not to mention their potential to rise higher.

Ironically, all you'd have to do to replenish those balloons and give them a fresh new start and appeal is to fill them back full of helium. If you did so on a regular basis, those balloons would last for months, bringing happiness and joy to all who saw them.

The same principle is true regarding our lives. Throughout the day, no matter how filled we are at the start, we "leak"; we get pressured or stressed; life happens. You get stuck in traffic, and a little helium goes out. You find out you didn't get the contract you were hoping for, and a little more escapes your balloon. You get home at the end of a hard day only to discover that your child is not feeling well, and you must deal with that. The dog got into the trash, you have to clean up that mess, and your balloon loses a little more of its shape.

The only way to stay full and to keep your joy and peace is to have a song of praise in your heart.

Today's Prayer to Become a Better You

Father, I thank You for this day. Thank You that I'm alive and healthy. Thank You for teaching me more and more to live each day with You.

Today's Thought to Become a Better You

Welcome, Holy Spirit, to every moment of this day.

A SMILING MELODY

You have given me greater joy than those who have abundant harvests of grain and new wine.

PSALM 4:7

I WONDER HOW MUCH more you and I would enjoy our lives if we would make melody in our hearts to God. How would our attitudes change if we did not take everything so seriously and refused to allow every setback or disappointment to depress us for two weeks. How much better our lives could be if we'd simply keep the song of praise in our hearts!

Maybe lately you have noticed that you don't smile as much as usual; you don't laugh much anymore. You have allowed the burdens of life to weigh you down. Perhaps you have settled into enduring your life and not really enjoying it. You don't have the fire and enthusiasm you once had.

This can all change, but it requires a decision on your part. You must develop some new habits. Number one: Develop a habit of smiling on purpose. "But I don't feel like smiling. I have a lot of problems, a lot of things coming against me," you might say.

No, sometimes you have to smile by faith. If you'll smile by faith, soon the joy will follow. Smiling sends a message to your whole body that everything is going to be okay. When you smile, chemicals are released throughout your physical system that make you feel better. Beyond that, when you smile, you'll have more of God's favor.

It will help you in your career. Smiling will help you in dealing with people. Numerous studies show that people who smile and are friendly, people who have a pleasant demeanor, get more breaks than other people who are solemn and unfriendly.

Somebody has said your smile is a million-dollar asset. If you're not using it, you're doing yourself a disservice. "Well, Joel, I don't think it matters whether I smile or not."

Develop a habit of smiling on purpose

God is concerned about your countenance. Fifty-three times in Scripture, He mentions it. When you smile, it's not only good for yourself, but it's a good witness to others. They will want the sort of happiness that you have. It's one thing to talk about our faith, but it's a far better thing to live it out. One of the best witnesses we could ever have is simply to be happy, to have a smile, to be friendly and pleasant to be around.

Today's Prayer to Become a Better You

Father, thank You for so many reasons to smile! Just the anticipation of what You can do in my life and in the lives of those I love brings joy to my heart and a smile to my face.

Today's Thought to Become a Better You

Knowing God's favor and character provokes smiles.

DECIDE TO SING

Despite all these things, overwhelming victory is ours through Christ, who loved us.

ROMANS 8:37

Declare today, "I'm not allowing another problem, another circumstance, or another person to keep me from giving God praise. I'm going to bless the Lord at all times. I'm going to get my song back."

I recognize that our problems are real and at times life is extremely difficult. But after you get through this problem, after you overcome this challenge, there will always be another challenge to overcome. There'll be something else to deal with. If you are waiting for all of your problems to go away before you decide to get your song back, you will miss the joy of living.

The apostle Paul had all sorts of difficulties, all kinds of challenges. But he said, "In all these things we are more than conquerors." Notice, he didn't say, "When these difficulties are done, I'm going to be happy." No, he said, "In the middle of this adversity, I'm going to enjoy my life anyway."

Number one: Get in a habit of smiling on purpose. Number two: Check your posture. Make sure you stand up tall, put your shoulders back, and hold your head up high. You are a child of the Most High God. You are not supposed to go around slumped over, feeling sloppy, weak, inferior, and thinking that you're unattractive.

Scripture says, "We are ambassadors of Christ." That means you represent Almighty God. Represent Him well. Even many good, godly people have gotten into a bad habit of slumping and looking down. When you do that, subconsciously you are communicating a lack of confidence, a lack of self-esteem. You need to put your shoulders back, hold your head up high, and communicate strength, determination, and confidence. Subconsciously, you're saying, *I'm proud of who I am. I know I'm made in the image of Almighty God. I know I am the apple of God's eye.*

If you are waiting for all of your problems to go away before you decide to get your song back, you will miss the joy of living.

 Today's Prayer to Become a Better You

Thank You for the song You gave me, Father. I can sing about what You have done for me no matter what's going on around me. You have made joy possible in every moment of life.

 Today's Thought to Become a Better You

I am an ambassador for Christ and a child of the King.

ANTICIPATION

SCRIPTURE READING TO BECOME A BETTER YOU   James 5:7–12

Dear brothers and sisters, be patient as you wait for the Lord's return. Consider the farmers who patiently wait for the rains in the fall and in the spring. They eagerly look for the valuable harvest to ripen.

JAMES 5:7

MUCH OF LIFE is spent waiting. There's a right way to wait and a wrong way. Too often when things don't happen on our timetable, we get down and discouraged. Even though we have the promise in our hearts, we give up and settle for the status quo. I believe it's because we're not waiting the right way.

The Bible says, "Be patient as you wait" (see James 5:7). Notice, it doesn't say if you wait, it says as you wait. The passage goes on to say, "See how the farmer waits expectantly." That's the key: We have to wait with expectancy. We're not supposed to sit around thinking, *My situation is never going to change. I prayed, I believed. But I don't see how I can ever get out of this mess.*

No, to wait with expectancy means that we are hopeful and positive. We get up every morning expecting good things. We may have problems, but we know this could be the day God turns it around. This could be the day I get the break I need.

Waiting should not be a passive thing. Waiting the correct way means you are on the lookout. You talk as if what you believe is going to happen. You act as though it's going to happen. You are making preparations.

If you are expecting someone for dinner, you don't wait until the guest shows up at your door before you prepare for the meal. Most likely you start early in the day. You make sure the house is clean. You may go to the grocery store the day before; perhaps you will buy some flowers for the table and swing by the bakery to get your favorite dessert—low-fat, of

We have to wait with expectancy.

course. You make all these preparations. Why? Because you're expecting someone.

We need a similar attitude while we're waiting for God's promises to come to pass. It's not enough merely to pray. We must put actions behind our prayers. Scripture says: "Faith without corresponding actions is dead" (see James 2:17). In other words, we can believe one way, we can talk one way, but if we're not putting the right actions behind our faith, it's not going to do any good.

Too often, we're believing one way, but actions are demonstrating the opposite—we're actually preparing for defeat. Maybe you come from a long line of divorces in your family. Instead of being afraid of ever getting married or worrying that your marriage will end in divorce, you need to start planning what you're going to do on your first wedding anniversary, and on your fifth anniversary, and on your twenty-fifth anniversary. Speak words of vitality and life regarding your marriage. Don't say, "I'm not sure our marriage is going to survive this strain." Not any of this, "If we make it, maybe we'll go on a cruise next year." Get rid of the "if" and start saying, "When we make it!"

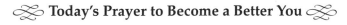

Today's Prayer to Become a Better You

Father, Your promises make it possible for me to live expec-

tantly. You have done, are doing, and are going to do great things for me. I can hardly wait for what's next!

⧼ Today's Thought to Become a Better You ⧽

I have permission to lean forward into God's favor.

PREPARE TO SUCCEED

It is impossible to please God without faith. Anyone who wants to come to him must believe that God exists and that he rewards those who sincerely seek him.

Hebrews 11:6

As you press on in life, stay hopeful and positive, and make preparations to succeed. We must understand there's a difference between believing and expecting. You can believe to have a child and not even be pregnant. But once you go from believing to expecting, you kick in to a different gear. When you are expecting, you'll furnish the nursery. You'll buy clothes for a baby that's not here yet. You'll call your friends and relatives and let them know the good news. "Mom! Dad! A baby is on its way." Even in the early stages of pregnancy, you start making all sorts of preparations. It affects your attitude, what you eat and drink, how you exercise, talk, and think.

You may go several months and say, "I look the same. I don't feel all that different." It doesn't matter what you see or feel. You received a report from the doctor that says a baby is on its way. That's all you need to know to start making preparations.

You need to do something similar when God puts a dream in your heart. Maybe one of His promises comes alive in your heart and mind, and for the first time, you dare to believe that your family can be restored. You know you can be healthy again. You know you can accomplish your dreams. The first thing is, you have to let the seed really take root. But you can't stop there. You must move on from believing to expecting.

"I'm doing that," you might say, "but I don't see anything happening. My finances aren't improving. I don't see any doors opening. My health is slipping rather than improving."

There's a difference between believing and expecting.

Scripture teaches, "We walk by faith, not by sight" (see 2 Corinthians 5:7). If you can see everything happening, you don't really need any faith. But when you have nothing to stand on in the natural—and you start acting as though God's Word is true, being positive and hopeful—you are putting actions behind your faith. That gets God's attention. That's what causes Him to work supernaturally in your life. What happened? You went from believing to expecting.

✖ Today's Prayer to Become a Better You ✖

When things don't happen instantly, Father, I want to keep trusting in You. I want to learn to walk by faith, not by sight, and I know You want to teach me to live that way. Thank You for wanting the best for me.

✖ Today's Thought to Become a Better You ✖

I'm expecting God to do something amazing today.

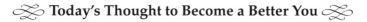

PRAYERFUL ACTION

We live by believing and not by seeing.
2 Corinthians 5:7

You get God's attention when you put actions behind your faith. Why not take a step of faith, plant a seed, do something that indicates to you and others that you are planning to succeed?

You may be facing sickness and disease. Maybe you've gotten some bad news concerning your health. Well, don't start planning your funeral. Don't sit around depressed, thinking about all the other people who have died from that same disease. Start making plans to get well.

When my father was preparing for open-heart surgery, it was an extremely serious situation. The doctors gave us no guarantees that it would turn out okay.

Instead of moping around in defeat, my father had us bring his tennis shoes and his running suit up to the hospital and put them right beside his bed. The facts said that he would not be up running anytime soon. But every day as he recovered, he'd look at those tennis shoes. In his mind, he was saying, One day soon, I'm going to be running again. One day I'm going to be healthy. One day I'm going to be strong. He was watering his seed, living expectantly, and that is what gave him the strength to carry on.

Scripture says, "Those who wait upon the LORD" (see Isaiah 40:31) will have their strength renewed. The Amplified Bible expands what it means to "wait on the LORD." It says, "Those . . . [who expect, look for, and hope in Him]." What might happen if we were to live with expectancy, stay hopeful, and make preparations for the goodness of God?

You get God's attention when you put actions behind your faith.

This Scripture goes on to say, "You will mount up with wings like the eagle. You will run and not get tired. You will walk and not faint." In other words, you will not stay down; you will overcome life's challenges.

If you can just get up every morning, expecting God to turn your problems around for good, if you can stay positive and hopeful, then God promises He will give you a supernatural strength that will cause you to soar like the eagle.

Remember, though, you need to put some actions behind your prayers. You may already be praying and believing; that's good. But don't stop there; keep pressing in closer to God. Move deeper to not only believing God can do something in your life but expecting that God will do great things in, for, and through you. Deliberately move from believing to expecting to receiving. Put action behind your faith. We cannot be passive and have God's best. When we're really expecting, we're on the lookout for opportunities. We're doing everything we can to make our dreams come to pass. Then God has an open invitation to pour out His favor in our lives.

Today's Prayer to Become a Better You

Father, thank You for clarifying my dreams and encouraging my expectations. Help me plan and prepare for what You will do in and through me. I want to live in active expectancy.

⤜ Today's Thought to Become a Better You ⤛

I will take a step of faith today based on my expectation to succeed.

PASSIONATE LIVING

Scripture Reading to Become a Better You   2 Timothy 4:1–8

*I have fought the good fight, I have finished the race,
and I have remained faithful.*

2 Timothy 4:7

If you want to become a better you, it is imperative that you appreciate the good things that God has done for you. Too many people have lost their passion for life. They've lost their enthusiasm. At one time, they were excited about their dreams. They got up every day with purpose and with passion. But now because of the time that's passed, the disappointments they have experienced, and the pressures of life, they're not excited about their dreams anymore. They've lost their fire.

At one time maybe you were excited about that person to whom you are married. You were so in love and so passionate, but now that relationship has become stale. You are going through the motions of life, getting up, going to work, coming home. But God does not want us to live that way. We should get up every day with enthusiasm, excited about that day. We should be grateful that we're alive, grateful for the opportunities in front of us, grateful for the people in our lives.

Understanding that most of life is rather routine, anything can become stagnant if we allow it to do so. You can have an exciting job, but it can become boring. Or you can be married to a fine, loving, caring person, but if you don't nourish that relationship and put something into it, over time, it is likely to get stagnant. We have to work at it if we're going to stay fresh. It doesn't automatically happen.

We need to stir ourselves up every day. The apostle Paul told Timothy, "Fan your flame." He was saying, "Timothy, don't let your fire go out. Stay passionate about your life. Stay enthusiastic about your dreams."

> Quit looking at what's wrong in your life, and start being grateful for what's right.

Maybe right now you are having difficulty being excited about your life, but keep your hope alive. You may have just a tiny flicker, and that fire is barely burning. You're about to give up on one of your dreams. Or maybe you're not excited about that relationship anymore. But the good news is, the fire is still in there, and if you will do your part to fan the flame, it can burst forth into passion once again. That means instead of dragging around finding every reason you can to be unhappy, you must change your focus. Quit looking at what's wrong in your life, and start being grateful for what's right in your life. Your attitude should be: "I am not going to live my life defeated and depressed. My dreams may not have come to pass yet; I may have some obstacles in my path, but I know God is still in control, I know He's got great things in store for me, so I'm going to get up each day excited about my life."

Everything may not be perfect in your life, but if you don't learn to be happy where you are, you will never get to where you want to be. You may not have the perfect job, but you should thank God that at least you are employed. Some people would love to have your job. Fan your flame and go to work with a new enthusiasm. Don't drag yourself into the workplace with a long face and then waste half the day playing on the Internet. Instead, give your employer 100 percent. Do your work with all your heart, to the best of your ability. Stay passionate about it. Everybody else may be slacking off;

everybody else may have sour attitudes. But you are not everybody else; you are a child of the Most High God. Don't be part of the problem; be part of the solution.

❧ Today's Prayer to Become a Better You ❧

Father, I am not going to live my life defeated and depressed. My dreams may not have come to pass yet; I may have some obstacles in my path, but I know You are still in control. I know You've got great things in store for me, so I'm going to get up each day excited about my life.

❧ Today's Thought to Become a Better You ❧

I can thank God every time I see something right today.

CATCH IT!

Scripture Reading to Become a Better You   Romans 12:9–16

Never be lazy, but work hard and serve the Lord enthusiastically.

Romans 12:11

Enthusiasm is contagious. If you go into your workplace with a smile on your face, full of life, full of joy, and full of victory, before long you'll rub off on others. That whole place will come up to a higher level, thanks to you.

The Bible says to "never lag in zeal, but be aglow and on fire serving the Lord" (see Romans 12:11). Do you get up each morning passionate about your dreams? Are you grateful for the home in which you live?

"Oh, I'm living in a tiny apartment," you may say. "I can't stand it. I want a bigger house."

No, you must learn to be happy right where you are. Understand that it dishonors God for us to go around complaining and thinking about everything that's wrong in our lives. You may not be living in your dream house, but you should thank God you have a roof over your head. Thank God you're not homeless, living out there in the elements.

"My husband and I don't have anything in common. We don't get along anymore."

Well, he may not be the perfect husband. But you can thank God that at least you have somebody to love. Do you know how many people are lonely today? Believe it or not, some woman would be glad to have your husband. Be grateful for that man. Be grateful for that woman.

We need to recognize that every day is a gift from God. What a shame to live any day with a negative and defeated mind-set.

**Every day
is a gift from God.**

Certainly, we all have obstacles in our paths and challenges to overcome, but our attitude should be, "Thank God, I'm alive. I live in a great country. I have family. I have opportunity. So I'm going to make the most of this day and give it my best."

"Well, Joel, I would do that, but I just found out I have to work late next week," or, "I have to go on a business trip," or, "I've got to take care of these kids all day."

No, you don't have to do anything; you *get to* do it. God is the one who has given you breath. You wouldn't be able to work late next week if God hadn't opened up that door of opportunity. You need to change your perspective. Don't do things out of obligation or because you have to—do them with an attitude of gratitude. In other words, "I don't have to go to work today; I get to go to work." "I don't have to take care of these children; they're a blessing; I get to take care of them." "I don't have to give; I get to give."

Scripture says, "When we are willing and obedient, we will eat the good of the land" (see Isaiah 1:19). It's one thing to be obedient. That's good. That's better than not being obedient. But if you really want to experience God's best, you need to be more than obedient; you have to be willing. You have to obey with the right attitude.

For instance, it's one thing to give because you have to. It's another thing to give because you want to. It's one thing to go to work to pick up a paycheck. It's another thing to go to work to be a blessing to somebody else. It's one thing to stay married to that person because it's the right thing to do. People may look down on you if you don't. But it's another thing to stay married to that person and to treat him or her with respect and honor and help your partner reach a higher level. That's being willing and obedient. When you do the right thing with the right motives, there's no limit to what God will do in your life. It is important that we get beyond mere obedience. That's easy, anybody can do that. To become a better you, take the next step and be willing to do the right thing with a good attitude.

Today's Prayer to Become a Better You

Thank You, Father, for the gift of enthusiasm. When I remember that You create every day and invite me to live in it to the fullest, I feel energized. I look forward to walking with You today!

Today's Thought to Become a Better You

Enthusiasm is one way for me to tell God "Thank You."

SURROUNDED BY MIRACLES

Scripture Reading to Become a Better You 1 Corinthians 2:1–12

No eye has seen, no ear has heard, and no mind has imagined what God has prepared for those who love him.

1 Corinthians 2:9

Miracles are all around us. The people in your life, the doors God has opened, the things that have happened along the way—they are not accidents. It was God's favor that caused you to be at the right place at the right time. You met someone and fell in love. Or you qualified for that home, and you know that by all usual means you would not have done so. Or you got that promotion unexpectedly. These are not coincidences. God was directing your steps, so don't take His blessings for granted.

What are you focused on today? Are you becoming a better you? Is there peace in your home and in your heart and mind? Are you happy, at rest, and enjoying life? We need to realize that this day is unique and irreplaceable. We need to make the most of it and live like it could be our last.

An elderly couple I knew were tremendous role models, always smiling and encouraging other people, and everyone loved them—especially the young people. Moreover, after decades of marriage, they still treated each other with honor and respect.

In her mid-eighties, the woman went home to be with the Lord. At the funeral, her husband, also an octogenarian, told an interesting story. He said, "About fifteen years ago, I had a heart attack. When my wife came to the hospital, she said, 'Honey, this just shows us how fragile life really is. You could have died.' She said, 'From now on, every night before we go to bed, I want us to kiss seven times just to show how much we love each other, just to show that we're not taking each other for granted.' And so, for these last fifteen or twenty years, we never went to sleep without kissing seven times."

**Miracles
are all around us.**

Don't you love that? That woman lived every day like it could be her last. She went to be with the Lord on a Tuesday, but Monday night, she kissed her husband seven times. Monday night, she told him how much she loved him. And when her life was over, she had no regrets. She made every day special. The last day of her life, she lived it loving, caring, at peace, and enjoying every moment. That's the way I want to live.

Friend, this day is a gift, so make the most of it. Shake off anything that hints of self-pity or discouragement, and find some reason to be grateful.

Becoming a better you is all in how you choose to view life. No matter what twists and turns life takes, you can find the good if you look for it. If we have the right attitude, we can see the sun shining even when it's cloudy. We can stay full of joy and keep getting better, even when things don't go our way.

My prayer is that God would give us a spirit of gratitude, that we'd always focus on the good and never take life for granted. If you will trust God each day and live according to His plan for your life, you will be happier and healthier, and you'll rise higher than you ever imagined possible.

Make a decision that you're going to live every day with enthusiasm. Get up each morning and think about all the things for which you can be grateful. If you need to, make a list. Keep it in front of you, and then go out each day pursuing your God-given dreams.

The Bible says to set your mind and keep it set on the higher things (see Colossians 3:2). I believe the higher things are the positive things, so first thing every day, set your mind in the right direction. Set your mind for success and victory. Set in your mind that you are going to enjoy this day. Then rise higher and get into the jet stream of God!

> Becoming a better you is all in how you choose to view life.

Remember, friend, you have seeds of greatness in you. You weren't made to be stagnant; rise out of complacency; keep growing, keep reaching for new heights. Your best days are still out in front of you.

You have not seen, heard, or imagined the great things God has in store for you. As you keep stretching to the next level, improving your life, and reaching for your highest potential, you will not only give birth to your dreams, but you will become a better you, better than you ever dreamed possible!

⚮ Today's Prayer to Become a Better You ⚮

Father, I acknowledge that I'm a miracle too. I'm a product of Your creative power, and I bear Your image. Thank You for filling my life with good and for filling me with such great hope for the future.

⚮ Today's Thought to Become a Better You ⚮

God is committed to making a better me out of me!